CHRIS DEVON

Asynchronous network Programming with python

First edition

This book was professionally typeset on Reedsy.
Find out more at reedsy.com

Contents

Understanding Asynchronous Programming

What is Asynchronous Programming?
Asynchronous programming is a programming paradigm that allows for the execution of tasks in a non-blocking manner. Unlike traditional synchronous programming, where operations are executed sequentially and can block the execution of subsequent tasks, asynchronous programming enables a program to initiate a task and move on to other tasks before the initial task is completed. This approach is particularly beneficial in environments where tasks involve waiting for external resources, such as network responses or file system operations, thereby improving the overall efficiency and responsiveness of applications.

Key Concepts in Asynchronous Programming
To grasp the concept of asynchronous programming, it is essential to understand several key terms and concepts:
Concurrency vs. Parallelism:

- **Concurrency** refers to the ability of a program to manage multiple tasks at once. These tasks may not necessarily be executing simultaneously; instead, they can be interleaved, with the program switching between tasks as needed.
- **Parallelism**, on the other hand, involves executing multiple tasks simultaneously, often on different processors or cores. While asyn-

chronous programming is primarily about concurrency, it can also facilitate parallel execution when combined with multi-threading or multi-processing.

Blocking vs. Non-Blocking Operations:

- **Blocking operations** halt the execution of a program until a task completes. For example, reading a file or making a network request typically blocks the program until the operation is finished, preventing any further execution in that thread.
- **Non-blocking operations**, however, allow the program to continue executing other tasks while waiting for a response. This is achieved by registering a callback or using a mechanism that notifies the program once the task completes.

Callbacks:

- A callback is a function that is passed as an argument to another function and is executed after the completion of the asynchronous task. Callbacks are a fundamental concept in asynchronous programming, enabling developers to specify what should happen once a task finishes.

Promises and Futures:

- Promises (or futures) are objects that represent the eventual completion (or failure) of an asynchronous operation. They provide a way to handle asynchronous results without deep nesting of callbacks, often referred to as "callback hell." Promises have states: pending, fulfilled, and rejected, allowing developers to chain operations and handle errors more gracefully.

Async/Await:

- In modern programming languages, including Python, the async/await syntax simplifies writing asynchronous code. By marking functions with async, developers indicate that these functions will perform asynchronous operations. The await keyword is then used to pause the execution of the async function until a promise is resolved, making the code appear more synchronous and readable.

Benefits of Asynchronous Programming

Asynchronous programming offers several advantages that make it an attractive choice for developers, particularly in networked and I/O-bound applications:

1. **Improved Performance**: By allowing tasks to run concurrently, asynchronous programming can significantly enhance the performance of applications, particularly when dealing with I/O-bound operations. This leads to better utilization of system resources, as the program does not waste time waiting for tasks to complete.
2. **Enhanced Responsiveness**: Applications that utilize asynchronous programming tend to be more responsive to user interactions. For example, in a graphical user interface (GUI) application, asynchronous operations ensure that the interface remains active while long-running tasks are processed in the background, preventing the application from freezing.
3. **Scalability**: Asynchronous programming is particularly beneficial for building scalable applications, such as web servers and microservices, where handling multiple requests concurrently is essential. By managing multiple tasks within a single thread, asynchronous applications can handle a larger number of simultaneous connections without the overhead of creating and managing multiple threads.
4. **Simplified Error Handling**: With the use of promises and the async/await syntax, error handling becomes more straightforward in asynchronous programming. Developers can catch errors at a higher level in the code, reducing complexity and improving maintainability.

When to Use Asynchronous Programming

While asynchronous programming offers numerous benefits, it is essential to recognize scenarios where it is most effective:

1. **I/O-Bound Operations**: Applications that rely heavily on I/O operations, such as reading from a database, making HTTP requests, or performing file operations, are prime candidates for asynchronous programming. These operations often involve waiting for external resources, making them ideal for a non-blocking approach.

2. **Event-Driven Applications**: Applications that respond to events, such as web servers or GUI applications, benefit from asynchronous programming. This paradigm allows them to handle multiple events without blocking the main thread, enhancing responsiveness and user experience.

3. **High-Throughput Systems**: Systems that require handling a large number of concurrent connections or requests, such as APIs or microservices, can leverage asynchronous programming to achieve higher throughput without the overhead of managing multiple threads.

4. **Resource-Constrained Environments**: In environments where resources such as memory or CPU are limited, asynchronous programming can help optimize resource usage by avoiding the overhead associated with creating and managing multiple threads or processes.

Asynchronous programming represents a powerful paradigm that enables developers to write more efficient, responsive, and scalable applications. By understanding its key concepts, benefits, and appropriate use cases, developers can harness the full potential of asynchronous programming to create applications that effectively manage concurrency and improve user experience.

As we delve deeper into this book, we will explore the specific tools and libraries in Python that facilitate asynchronous programming, along with hands-on projects that demonstrate these principles in action. By the end of this journey, you will not only understand the theory behind asynchronous programming but also possess the practical skills to implement it effectively in your own projects.

Benefits of Asynchronous Programming

Asynchronous programming is gaining popularity across various domains due to its capacity to enhance performance and user experience in applications. Understanding the specific benefits of this programming paradigm is crucial for developers looking to leverage its full potential. Below, we delve into the key advantages that asynchronous programming offers:

1. Improved Performance

One of the most significant benefits of asynchronous programming is its ability to improve application performance, particularly in I/O-bound scenarios. Traditional synchronous operations can lead to idle CPU time when a program is waiting for a response from an external source, such as a database or a web service. This waiting can become a bottleneck, reducing the overall efficiency of the application.

By adopting an asynchronous approach, a program can initiate an I/O operation and immediately proceed to execute other tasks while awaiting the response. This non-blocking behavior enables better resource utilization, as the CPU can work on other computations instead of remaining idle. Consequently, applications can handle more requests in a given timeframe, making them faster and more efficient.

2. Enhanced Responsiveness

In user-facing applications, responsiveness is critical for providing a seamless experience. Traditional synchronous programming often leads to situations where an application becomes unresponsive while waiting for a long-running task to complete. For instance, when a user submits a form that triggers a lengthy database query, the entire application may freeze until the query finishes.

Asynchronous programming mitigates this issue by allowing the application to remain responsive. By executing long-running tasks in the background, the application can continue to process user inputs and update the user interface. This leads to a smoother user experience, reducing frustration and improving overall satisfaction.

3. Scalability

Asynchronous programming is particularly advantageous for building scalable applications. In scenarios where a server must handle numerous concurrent connections, such as web servers or microservices, the traditional multi-threaded approach can become cumbersome. Each connection typically requires a dedicated thread, which consumes system resources and can lead to overhead as the number of connections increases.

With asynchronous programming, a single thread can manage multiple connections without the need for additional threads. This ability to handle thousands of simultaneous connections using fewer resources allows applications to scale efficiently. As a result, businesses can accommodate higher traffic without significantly increasing infrastructure costs.

4. Resource Efficiency

Resource efficiency is another crucial benefit of asynchronous programming. In environments where CPU and memory resources are constrained, such as embedded systems or mobile applications, minimizing resource consumption becomes essential. Traditional synchronous approaches may lead to excessive resource usage, particularly if many threads are created and managed simultaneously.

Asynchronous programming reduces the resource footprint by allowing the application to perform non-blocking operations. This approach enables a single-threaded model to handle multiple tasks effectively, resulting in lower memory overhead and reduced context-switching costs. Consequently, applications can run more efficiently on limited hardware.

5. Simplified Error Handling

Error handling in asynchronous programming has evolved significantly with the introduction of modern languages that support promises and async/await constructs. In traditional callback-based approaches, handling errors often involves deeply nested callbacks, making the code difficult to read and maintain.

With promises and async/await, developers can handle errors more intuitively. The try/catch blocks can be used around await statements to catch exceptions that may arise from asynchronous operations. This clearer structure allows developers to write cleaner, more maintainable code while effectively managing error scenarios.

6. Better Management of Long-Running Tasks

Asynchronous programming is particularly effective in scenarios involving long-running tasks. For example, in applications that require extensive data processing, such as image or video processing, performing these tasks synchronously can result in significant delays and resource consumption.

By executing these tasks asynchronously, developers can allow the application to remain responsive to user actions while the processing occurs in the background. This approach is beneficial in ensuring that the application remains functional and user-friendly, even when dealing with computationally intensive operations.

7. Flexibility in Application Design

Asynchronous programming promotes flexibility in application design. Developers can choose to implement asynchronous logic where it is most beneficial, such as in handling I/O operations or in specific components of a system. This modular approach enables teams to build more versatile applications that can adapt to varying workloads and requirements.

Moreover, asynchronous patterns can be combined with other programming paradigms, such as reactive programming, to create even more sophisticated architectures. This flexibility empowers developers to adopt the best approach for their specific use cases, leading to more robust and adaptable applications.

8. Improved User Experience

In a world where user expectations are continually rising, providing a positive user experience is paramount. Asynchronous programming allows applications to deliver a more engaging experience by minimizing waiting times and ensuring that users can interact with the application seamlessly.

By providing feedback to users during long operations—such as loading spinners or progress indicators—developers can enhance the perceived performance of the application. This positive reinforcement encourages user engagement and satisfaction, ultimately contributing to a more successful product.

Asynchronous programming offers a range of compelling benefits that can significantly enhance the performance, scalability, and user experience of applications. By understanding these advantages, developers can make informed decisions about when and how to implement asynchronous patterns in their projects.

When to Use Asynchronous Programming

Asynchronous programming is a powerful paradigm that excels in specific contexts, particularly in scenarios involving I/O-bound operations and the need for high responsiveness. However, it is not a one-size-fits-all solution. Understanding when to employ asynchronous programming is critical for maximizing its benefits while avoiding unnecessary complexity. Below, we outline the key situations in which asynchronous programming is particularly advantageous.

1. I/O-Bound Operations

I/O-bound operations are those that require waiting for external resources, such as network responses, disk access, or database queries. These operations often involve significant waiting time, during which the CPU would typically remain idle in a synchronous model. Asynchronous programming is especially beneficial in these scenarios because it allows the program to initiate an I/O operation and continue executing other tasks without waiting.

Examples of I/O-bound operations include:

- **Network Requests**: Making API calls or fetching data from remote servers can introduce latency. By using asynchronous programming, you can initiate these requests and handle other tasks while waiting for the response.
- **File I/O**: Reading from or writing to disk can be slow, especially with large files. Asynchronous file operations enable the application to remain responsive while performing these tasks.
- **Database Queries**: Querying databases often involves waiting for results. Asynchronous database clients can help manage multiple queries without blocking the application.

2. Event-Driven Applications

Event-driven applications, such as web servers or GUI applications, require responsiveness to user interactions and events. In these contexts, asynchronous programming allows the application to handle multiple events without blocking the main thread, ensuring that user interfaces remain responsive and capable of processing user input efficiently.

Scenarios in event-driven applications include:

- **Web Servers**: In web applications, a server must respond to multiple incoming requests simultaneously. Asynchronous programming enables the server to handle numerous requests concurrently, enhancing throughput and performance.
- **Graphical User Interfaces**: GUI applications often need to perform background operations while allowing users to interact with the interface. Asynchronous programming keeps the UI responsive, enabling users to continue working without interruption.

3. High-Throughput Systems

High-throughput systems are designed to handle a large volume of requests or data streams. Asynchronous programming is ideal for these systems because it minimizes the overhead associated with managing multiple threads or processes. Instead, a single thread can manage numerous connections efficiently.

Common applications include:

- **Real-Time Data Processing**: Applications that process streams of data, such as social media feeds or sensor data, benefit from asynchronous programming to handle incoming data without delay.
- **Microservices Architectures**: In microservices, services often communicate over the network. Asynchronous programming enables services to interact without blocking each other, improving overall system performance.

4. Resource-Constrained Environments

In environments where system resources such as memory and CPU are limited, optimizing resource usage is crucial. Asynchronous programming helps minimize resource consumption by allowing a single-threaded model to manage multiple tasks efficiently, avoiding the overhead associated with multi-threading.

Typical scenarios include:

- **Embedded Systems**: Devices with limited processing power and memory can benefit from asynchronous programming to handle multiple tasks without overwhelming the hardware.
- **Mobile Applications**: Mobile devices often have constrained resources. Asynchronous programming can help ensure that applications run smoothly while minimizing battery consumption.

5. Long-Running Tasks

Asynchronous programming is well-suited for managing long-running tasks that might otherwise block the application. By executing these tasks asynchronously, developers can ensure that the application remains functional and user-friendly, even when dealing with computationally intensive operations.

Examples of long-running tasks include:

- **Data Processing**: Tasks such as data transformation or analysis can take significant time to complete. By running these operations in the background, the application can provide progress updates and remain interactive.
- **Batch Jobs**: Applications that need to process large batches of data can leverage asynchronous programming to manage these jobs without impacting user experience.

6. Scalability Requirements

When building applications that need to scale efficiently, asynchronous programming can be a game-changer. By allowing a single thread to manage multiple tasks, developers can build systems that can grow to accommodate increasing user demands without a proportional increase in resource consumption.

Situations where scalability is crucial include:

- **Web Applications**: As user traffic increases, asynchronous programming can help maintain performance levels without requiring extensive infrastructure changes.
- **Cloud-Native Applications**: In cloud environments, where scalability is often a requirement, asynchronous programming facilitates the development of applications that can respond to fluctuating workloads dynamically.

7. User Experience Optimization

In user-facing applications, providing a positive user experience is paramount. Asynchronous programming helps create applications that are responsive and engaging, allowing users to interact seamlessly with the application while background processes are running.

User experience scenarios include:

- **Form Submissions**: When users submit forms that trigger long-running processes, asynchronous programming can provide immediate feedback, such as loading indicators or success messages, without freezing the interface.
- **Dynamic Content Loading**: Applications that load content dynamically, such as infinite scrolling features, benefit from asynchronous programming to retrieve data without disrupting the user experience.

Asynchronous programming is a powerful tool that can significantly enhance the performance and user experience of applications in various contexts. By understanding the specific scenarios in which asynchronous programming excels—such as I/O-bound operations, event-driven applications, high-throughput systems, resource-constrained environments, long-running tasks, scalability requirements, and user experience optimization—developers can make informed decisions about when to implement this paradigm in their projects.

Key Concepts and Terminology

Understanding asynchronous programming requires familiarity with several key concepts and terminology that form the foundation of this paradigm. Each term represents a fundamental idea that contributes to the overall functionality and effectiveness of asynchronous programming. Below, we break down these concepts to provide clarity and context for their application in programming.

1. Concurrency

Concurrency is the ability of a program to manage multiple tasks simultaneously. In a concurrent system, tasks can progress without waiting for each other to complete. It's important to note that concurrency does not necessarily imply parallelism; tasks may not be executed at the same time but can be interleaved to create the illusion of simultaneous execution.

For example, in a web server, multiple client requests can be handled concurrently. Even if only one request is processed at a time, the server can switch between requests, making it appear as if all requests are being handled simultaneously.

2. Blocking vs. Non-Blocking Operations

- **Blocking Operations**: These operations halt the execution of the program until the task is completed. For example, when a program performs a synchronous network request, it cannot do anything else until it receives a response. This waiting can lead to inefficiencies, especially in applications that require responsiveness.
- **Non-Blocking Operations**: In contrast, non-blocking operations allow a program to initiate a task and continue executing other code while waiting for the task to complete. Non-blocking operations are essential for building responsive applications, as they prevent the program from becoming unresponsive during long-running tasks.

3. Callbacks

A callback is a function that is passed as an argument to another function and is executed once a particular task is complete. Callbacks are a foundational concept in asynchronous programming, allowing developers to specify what should happen after an asynchronous operation finishes.

For instance, when making an asynchronous HTTP request, a callback function can be defined to process the response once it arrives. While callbacks are powerful, they can lead to complex, nested code structures known as "callback hell," making it harder to read and maintain.

4. Promises and Futures

Promises and futures are abstractions that represent the eventual completion or failure of an asynchronous operation. They provide a way to handle asynchronous results without deeply nested callbacks.

- **Promises**: A promise is an object that can be in one of three states: pending, fulfilled, or rejected. A promise starts in a pending state and transitions to either fulfilled (when the operation completes successfully) or rejected (if an error occurs). Promises can be chained using .then() and .catch() methods, allowing for cleaner handling of results and errors.
- **Futures**: Similar to promises, futures represent a value that may be available in the future. In some languages, futures are used interchangeably with promises, but the term "future" often emphasizes the aspect of delayed computation.

5. Async/Await

The async/await syntax is a modern feature in many programming languages, including Python, that simplifies the process of writing asynchronous code. This syntax allows developers to write asynchronous operations in a way that resembles synchronous code, making it easier to read and maintain.

- **Async Functions**: Functions defined with the async keyword are asynchronous and can contain await expressions. When an async function is called, it returns a promise that resolves when the function completes.
- **Await Expressions**: The await keyword is used to pause the execution of an async function until the promise is resolved. This allows the code to execute in a sequential manner, enhancing readability without sacrificing the benefits of asynchronous execution.

6. Event Loop

The event loop is a core component of asynchronous programming that enables the management of asynchronous tasks. It continually checks for and executes tasks, allowing a program to handle multiple operations without blocking.

When an asynchronous operation is initiated, it is added to the event loop. The loop processes tasks, including I/O operations, timers, and callbacks, in a non-blocking manner. If a task is waiting for a resource (like a network response), the event loop can switch to another task, maintaining application responsiveness.

7. Tasks and Scheduling

In asynchronous programming, a task represents an individual unit of work that the event loop manages. Tasks can be scheduled for execution when resources become available or when a specific event occurs.

- **Task Scheduling**: The event loop schedules tasks based on their readiness. If a task is waiting for a response from a network call, it is placed in a pending state until the response is received. Once ready, the task is executed, often in the order it was scheduled.

8. Cooperative Multitasking

Cooperative multitasking is a technique in which tasks voluntarily yield control to allow other tasks to run. In the context of asynchronous programming, this means that a running task must explicitly indicate when it is willing to pause its execution (usually with an await statement) to let other tasks proceed. This approach is essential in preventing a single task from monopolizing resources and ensures a fair execution order.

9. Race Conditions

Race conditions occur when the outcome of an operation depends on the relative timing of events, particularly in concurrent environments. In asynchronous programming, race conditions can arise if multiple tasks attempt to access shared resources simultaneously without proper synchronization. This can lead to unpredictable behavior and bugs that are often difficult to diagnose and fix.

Developers must be mindful of race conditions when designing asynchronous systems, employing techniques such as locking mechanisms or using atomic operations to ensure data consistency.

10. Cancellation

Cancellation is an important aspect of asynchronous programming, allowing developers to stop or abort ongoing asynchronous operations if they are no longer needed. This can improve resource management and application responsiveness, particularly in user-driven applications where actions may change based on user input.

To support cancellation, programming frameworks may provide constructs such as cancellable promises or tokens that signal when an operation should be aborted.

Familiarity with the key concepts and terminology associated with asynchronous programming is crucial for understanding how to implement this paradigm effectively. By grasping terms such as concurrency, blocking vs. non-blocking operations, callbacks, promises, async/await, the event loop, and others, developers can better navigate the complexities of asynchronous programming.

Getting Started with Python's Asyncio

Installing Python and Required Libraries

Before diving into asynchronous programming with Python's asyncio library, it's essential to set up your development environment correctly. This chapter guides you through the installation of Python and the necessary libraries to start building asynchronous applications.

Step 1: Installing Python

To begin, you need to have Python installed on your system. Python is a versatile programming language that supports various paradigms, including asynchronous programming. The following steps will help you install Python on different operating systems:

Downloading Python

Visit the Official Python Website: Go to the Python Downloads page.

Choose the Version: Download the latest stable version of Python. As of this writing, Python 3.x is the recommended version for new projects, as Python 2 has reached its end of life.

Select Your Operating System: The website automatically detects your operating system (Windows, macOS, or Linux) and suggests the appropriate installer. You can also choose the version that matches your system architecture (32-bit or 64-bit).

Installing Python

Windows:

Run the downloaded installer.

Check "Add Python to PATH": This option is crucial as it allows you to run Python from the command line without specifying the full path.

Select "Install Now" for a standard installation, or choose "Customize Installation" if you want to modify the installation options.

Follow the prompts to complete the installation.

macOS:

Run the downloaded .pkg file.

Follow the prompts in the installation wizard.

Alternatively, you can use Homebrew, a package manager for macOS, by running:

```bash

brew install python
```

Linux:

Most Linux distributions come with Python pre-installed. To check if Python is already installed, open a terminal and run:

```bash

python3 --version
```

If it is not installed, you can install Python using the package manager for your distribution. For example, on Ubuntu, you can run:

```bash

sudo apt update
sudo apt install python3
```

Verifying the Installation

Once Python is installed, you can verify the installation by opening a command prompt or terminal and running:

```bash
python --version
```

or for systems that use python3:

```bash
python3 --version
```

This command should display the installed version of Python. Additionally, you can start the Python interactive shell by simply typing python or python3 in your terminal.

Step 2: Setting Up a Virtual Environment

Using a virtual environment is a best practice for managing dependencies in Python projects. Virtual environments create isolated spaces for your project, ensuring that dependencies do not interfere with each other. Here's how to set up a virtual environment:

Creating a Virtual Environment

Navigate to Your Project Directory: Use the terminal to navigate to the folder where you want to create your project.

```bash
cd /path/to/your/project
```

Create the Virtual Environment: Run the following command:

```bash
python -m venv venv
```

This command creates a new directory named venv that contains a copy of the Python interpreter and a fresh installation of the standard library.

Activating the Virtual Environment

After creating a virtual environment, you need to activate it to start using it:

- **Windows**:

```bash
venv\Scripts\activate
```

- **macOS and Linux**:

```bash
source venv/bin/activate
```

Once activated, your terminal prompt should change to indicate that you are working within the virtual environment.

Deactivating the Virtual Environment

To exit the virtual environment, simply run:

```bash
deactivate
```

This command will return you to the system's default Python environment.

Step 3: Installing Required Libraries

Now that Python and the virtual environment are set up, it's time to install the libraries needed for asynchronous programming with asyncio. While Python's standard library includes asyncio, there are other useful libraries that enhance asynchronous programming capabilities.

Installing asyncio

If you are using Python 3.3 or later, asyncio comes pre-installed as part of the standard library. You can verify its availability by running:

```python
import asyncio
print(asyncio.__version__)
```

This should display the version number of asyncio. If you receive an import error, ensure that you have Python 3.3 or later installed.

Additional Libraries

While asyncio is powerful on its own, you might want to use additional libraries that work seamlessly with it. Here are some popular libraries that can enhance your asynchronous programming experience:

- **Aiohttp**: A powerful HTTP client and server framework for asynchronous programming.

```bash
bash
```

```bash
pip install aiohttp
```

- **Asyncio-Redis**: An asynchronous Redis client that allows you to interact with Redis databases.

```bash
bash
```

```bash
pip install aioredis
```

- **Motor**: An asynchronous driver for MongoDB that uses asyncio.

```bash
bash
```

```bash
pip install motor
```

- **FastAPI**: A modern web framework for building APIs with Python, based on Starlette and Pydantic, which supports asynchronous programming natively.

```bash
bash
```

```bash
pip install fastapi
```

- **SQLAlchemy**: While SQLAlchemy is traditionally synchronous, it has an asynchronous extension that allows for non-blocking database interactions.

```bash
pip install sqlalchemy[asyncio]
```

Installing Packages

Once you have identified the libraries you want to install, use the pip command to install them within your activated virtual environment. For example:

```bash
pip install aiohttp fastapi
```

You can check installed packages with:

```bash
pip list
```

Step 4: Writing Your First Asynchronous Program

With Python and the required libraries installed, you can now write your first asynchronous program using asyncio. Here's a simple example to demonstrate the basic usage of asyncio:

```python
import asyncio

async def greet(name):
```

```
    await asyncio.sleep(1)  # Simulating an I/O-bound operation
    print(f"Hello, {name}!")

async def main():
    await asyncio.gather(
        greet("Alice"),
        greet("Bob"),
        greet("Charlie"),
    )

if __name__ == "__main__":
    asyncio.run(main())
```

This program defines an asynchronous function greet that simulates a delay (representing an I/O operation) and then prints a greeting. The main function uses asyncio.gather to run multiple greet calls concurrently. When executed, it will greet all names with a one-second delay, demonstrating the efficiency of asynchronous programming.

In this chapter, we have covered the essential steps for setting up your development environment for asynchronous programming with Python's asyncio. We discussed installing Python, creating and managing virtual environments, and installing required libraries. With this foundation in place, you are now prepared to explore the powerful features of asyncio and start building asynchronous applications.

Introduction to the Asyncio Library

The asyncio library is a powerful and versatile framework in Python that provides a structured way to write concurrent code using the async/await syntax. Introduced in Python 3.3 and significantly enhanced in subsequent releases, asyncio simplifies the development of asynchronous applications by managing asynchronous tasks, events, and I/O operations without the need for complex threading or callback structures. This section provides an overview of the asyncio library, its key features, and how it fits into the broader context of asynchronous programming.

Overview of Asyncio

At its core, asyncio is designed to facilitate the development of applications that require non-blocking I/O operations, such as network communication, file handling, and inter-process communication. The library is built around the concept of an event loop, which acts as a central coordinator for executing asynchronous tasks.

Here are some of the fundamental components of asyncio:

1. **Event Loop**: The heart of the asyncio library, the event loop is responsible for executing asynchronous tasks and managing their execution order. It continuously checks for tasks that are ready to run and processes them accordingly.
2. **Coroutines**: Coroutines are special functions defined using the async def syntax. They can contain await expressions, which allow the coroutine to yield control back to the event loop while waiting for an asynchronous operation to complete. This makes it possible to write code that appears sequential but operates asynchronously.
3. **Tasks**: A task is a coroutine that has been scheduled for execution in the event loop. asyncio allows you to create tasks using the asyncio.cr eate_task() function or the loop.create_task() method. Once created, tasks can run concurrently, allowing multiple operations to progress without blocking each other.
4. **Futures**: A future is an object that represents a result that may not be available yet. Futures are used to manage the results of asynchronous operations. In asyncio, futures are typically created when a coroutine is scheduled, and they can be awaited to retrieve the result once the operation is complete.
5. **Synchronization Primitives**: asyncio provides several synchronization primitives, such as events, locks, and semaphores, to manage concurrent access to shared resources. These primitives help prevent race conditions and ensure data integrity in asynchronous applications.

Key Features of Asyncio

The asyncio library is packed with features that make it an essential tool for asynchronous programming in Python. Here are some of the key features:

1. **Ease of Use with Async/Await**: The introduction of the async/await syntax in Python has greatly simplified the writing and reading of asynchronous code. Developers can write asynchronous functions that resemble synchronous code, enhancing readability and maintainability.

2. **Efficient I/O Handling**: asyncio is built for efficient handling of I/O-bound tasks. It uses non-blocking sockets and operates on the event loop, which allows for multiple I/O operations to be initiated and handled concurrently without blocking the program's execution.

3. **Concurrency with Coroutine Scheduling**: asyncio allows developers to schedule multiple coroutines for execution. With functions like asyncio.gather(), you can run multiple coroutines concurrently and wait for them to complete, managing complex workflows with ease.

4. **Support for Asynchronous Networking**: The library provides built-in support for networking tasks, including HTTP clients and servers. With asyncio, developers can build high-performance network applications capable of handling numerous simultaneous connections.

5. **Error Handling**: asyncio simplifies error handling in asynchronous code. Using try and except blocks within coroutines allows developers to catch and handle exceptions gracefully, making debugging easier.

6. **Interoperability with Existing Libraries**: asyncio is designed to work well with existing Python libraries and frameworks. Many popular libraries, such as aiohttp, FastAPI, and SQLAlchemy, integrate seamlessly with asyncio, allowing developers to leverage its features in their projects.

7. **Built-in Task Management**: The library provides facilities for managing tasks, including cancellation and timeout mechanisms. Tasks can be cancelled gracefully, and developers can set timeouts for operations to avoid long waits for unresponsive tasks.

Basic Components of Asyncio

To effectively use asyncio, it is important to familiarize yourself with its basic components:

Creating and Running an Event Loop: The event loop is the central component of asyncio. You can run the default event loop using:

```python
import asyncio

asyncio.run(main())
```

In this example, main() is the entry point for the asynchronous code.

Defining Coroutines: Coroutines are defined using the async def syntax. Within these coroutines, you can use await to pause execution until an awaited task completes:

```python
async def my_coroutine():
    await asyncio.sleep(1)  # Simulates an asynchronous operation
    print("Task completed!")
```

Scheduling Tasks: To schedule a coroutine for execution, you can use asyncio.create_task():

```python
task = asyncio.create_task(my_coroutine())
```

Waiting for Tasks to Complete: To wait for multiple tasks to finish, you can use asyncio.gather():

```python
python
```

```python
async def main():
    await asyncio.gather(my_coroutine(), another_coroutine())
```

Handling Exceptions: Error handling in coroutines can be done with traditional try/except blocks:

```python
python
```

```python
async def faulty_coroutine():
    try:
        await some_async_operation()
    except Exception as e:
        print(f"An error occurred: {e}")
```

The asyncio library is a foundational tool for writing asynchronous code in Python, enabling developers to build efficient, high-performance applications that can handle multiple tasks concurrently. Its design principles and features cater to the needs of modern software development, making it a valuable addition to any Python developer's toolkit.

Understanding the Event Loop

The event loop is a core component of the asyncio library and serves as the backbone of asynchronous programming in Python. It orchestrates the execution of asynchronous tasks, manages their scheduling, and handles events in a non-blocking manner. In this section, we will explore the event loop's architecture, its role in asynchronous programming, how it operates, and its interaction with coroutines and tasks.

What is an Event Loop?

An event loop is a programming construct that waits for and dispatches events or messages in a program. It runs in a single thread and continually checks for events that need to be processed. In the context of asyncio, the event loop is responsible for executing asynchronous functions (coroutines), managing I/O operations, and coordinating the flow of control between different tasks.

Key Responsibilities of the Event Loop

1. **Task Scheduling**: The event loop schedules coroutines and other asynchronous operations for execution. It manages the lifecycle of tasks, including starting, pausing, and resuming them as necessary.
2. **Event Handling**: The event loop listens for events, such as I/O operations completing or timers expiring. When an event occurs, the loop invokes the appropriate callback or resumes the corresponding coroutine.
3. **Non-blocking Execution**: By utilizing a non-blocking model, the event loop allows other tasks to run while waiting for I/O operations to complete. This capability is essential for building responsive applications that can handle multiple concurrent operations.
4. **Error Management**: The event loop also provides mechanisms for handling errors in coroutines and tasks. It can catch exceptions raised during the execution of asynchronous operations, allowing developers to implement appropriate error-handling strategies.

How the Event Loop Works

The operation of the event loop can be broken down into several stages:

Initialization: When you start an asyncio program, the event loop is initialized. In most cases, you can use asyncio.run() to start the event loop and run your main coroutine.

```python

import asyncio
```

```
async def main():
    print("Hello, Asyncio!")

asyncio.run(main())
```

Task Creation: As the program runs, coroutines are defined and scheduled for execution as tasks. The event loop manages these tasks using the asyncio.create_task() function or loop.create_task() method.

```python
async def task1():
    await asyncio.sleep(1)
    print("Task 1 completed")

async def task2():
    await asyncio.sleep(2)
    print("Task 2 completed")

asyncio.create_task(task1())
asyncio.create_task(task2())
```

1. **Running the Loop**: The event loop begins executing tasks in a cooperative multitasking manner. When a coroutine encounters an await statement, control is yielded back to the event loop, allowing it to execute other tasks while waiting for the awaited operation to complete.
2. **Event Handling**: The event loop continuously checks for events. If an I/O operation completes (for example, data is received from a network connection), the event loop will invoke the corresponding callback or resume the awaiting coroutine.
3. **Task Completion**: Once a task is completed, its result is returned to the calling coroutine. If the task raised an exception, the event loop can catch it, and developers can handle it appropriately.

4. **Exiting the Loop**: The event loop runs until all tasks have been completed. When there are no more tasks to execute, the loop stops, and the program exits.

The Lifecycle of a Coroutine

Understanding how coroutines interact with the event loop is crucial for effective asynchronous programming. Here's a simplified lifecycle of a coroutine:

1. **Creation**: A coroutine is defined using the async def syntax.
2. **Scheduling**: The coroutine is scheduled as a task using asyncio.create _task() or loop.create_task().
3. **Execution**: The event loop begins executing the coroutine. When the coroutine reaches an await statement, it yields control back to the event loop.
4. **Awaiting**: The event loop continues to run and can process other tasks while waiting for the awaited operation to finish.
5. **Completion**: Once the awaited operation is complete, the event loop resumes the coroutine, allowing it to continue executing until it reaches another await or completes.
6. **Finalization**: Upon completion, the result of the coroutine is returned, or an exception is raised if one occurred.

Using the Event Loop Directly

While asyncio.run() is the most common way to start the event loop, developers can also interact with the event loop directly. Here's an example of how to do that:

```python
import asyncio

async def greet(name):
```

```
    await asyncio.sleep(1)
    print(f"Hello, {name}!")

# Get the current event loop
loop = asyncio.get_event_loop()

try:
    # Schedule the coroutines
    loop.run_until_complete(asyncio.gather(greet("Alice"),
    greet("Bob")))
finally:
    # Close the loop
    loop.close()
```

In this example, we first retrieve the current event loop using asyncio.get_e vent_loop(), then schedule multiple coroutines using loop.run_until_compl ete(). Finally, we close the loop to free up resources.

Best Practices for Working with the Event Loop

To effectively use the event loop in your asynchronous applications, consider the following best practices:

1. **Use asyncio.run()**: For most applications, prefer using asyncio.run() to manage the event loop automatically. It simplifies the management of resources and eliminates the need for explicit loop closure.
2. **Avoid Blocking Calls**: Ensure that your coroutines do not contain blocking calls (like time.sleep() or synchronous I/O operations). Use non-blocking equivalents, such as await asyncio.sleep().
3. **Handle Exceptions Gracefully**: Use try/except blocks within your coroutines to manage exceptions effectively. This practice helps to ensure that errors do not go unhandled and allows for better debugging.
4. **Limit Long-Running Tasks**: Avoid performing long-running com- putations directly in the event loop. Instead, consider using thread pools or separate processes to handle CPU-bound tasks.
5. **Keep the Event Loop Running**: Make sure that the event loop

remains active while you have outstanding tasks. If the loop exits prematurely, any pending tasks will be discarded.

6. **Utilize Task Groups**: In Python 3.11 and later, consider using asyncio.TaskGroup for managing tasks more effectively, providing a context manager to wait for a group of tasks to complete while handling exceptions.

The event loop is a fundamental component of the asyncio library, enabling the execution of asynchronous tasks in a non-blocking manner. By managing the scheduling and execution of coroutines, the event loop plays a critical role in building efficient, high-performance applications. Understanding how the event loop operates, its lifecycle, and best practices for its use will empower you to develop robust asynchronous programs in Python.

Writing Your First Asyncio Program

With a solid understanding of the asyncio library and the event loop, it's time to put that knowledge into practice by writing your first asynchronous program. In this section, we will walk through the process of creating a simple yet effective asyncio application that demonstrates the core concepts and features of the library.

Program Overview

We will develop a basic program that simulates multiple concurrent tasks, such as fetching data from different sources (simulated with delays) and processing that data. This example will highlight how to use coroutines, the event loop, and asynchronous operations effectively.

Step 1: Setting Up the Project

Before we start coding, make sure you have Python installed and that you're working in a virtual environment with the asyncio library (which is part of the standard library in Python 3.x). You do not need to install it separately.

You can create a new Python file called asyncio_example.py in your project directory.

Step 2: Writing the Asynchronous Program

Below is the complete code for a simple asyncio program that fetches and processes data concurrently. The program simulates fetching data from different sources using asynchronous functions:

```python
import asyncio
import random

async def fetch_data(source_id):
    """Simulates fetching data from an external source."""
    print(f"Starting to fetch data from source {source_id}...")
    # Simulate a random network delay (1 to 3 seconds)
    await asyncio.sleep(random.randint(1, 3))
    data = f"Data from source {source_id}"
    print(f"Completed fetching data from source {source_id}.")
    return data

async def process_data(data):
    """Simulates processing the fetched data."""
    print(f"Processing {data}...")
    # Simulate processing time (1 to 2 seconds)
    await asyncio.sleep(random.randint(1, 2))
    print(f"Finished processing {data}.")
    return f"Processed {data}"

async def main():
    # Create a list to hold the tasks
    fetch_tasks = []

    # Create fetch tasks for multiple sources
    for i in range(5):  # Simulating 5 data sources
        task = asyncio.create_task(fetch_data(i))
```

```
        fetch_tasks.append(task)

    # Wait for all fetch tasks to complete
    fetched_data = await asyncio.gather(*fetch_tasks)

    # Process the fetched data concurrently
    process_tasks = []
    for data in fetched_data:
        task = asyncio.create_task(process_data(data))
        process_tasks.append(task)

    # Wait for all processing tasks to complete
    await asyncio.gather(*process_tasks)

if __name__ == "__main__":
    asyncio.run(main())
```

Explanation of the Code

Importing Required Modules: We import the asyncio library and the random module to simulate varying delays in fetching and processing data.

Defining the fetch_data Coroutine:

- This asynchronous function simulates fetching data from an external source identified by source_id.
- It prints a message indicating the start of data fetching.
- It uses await asyncio.sleep() to simulate a network delay, which represents the time it takes to fetch data.
- After the delay, it returns the fetched data.

Defining the process_data Coroutine:

- This asynchronous function simulates processing the data fetched from the sources.
- It prints a message indicating the start of data processing.
- Similar to the fetching function, it uses await asyncio.sleep() to simulate processing time.

- After processing, it returns a message indicating the processed data.

Defining the main Coroutine:

- This is the main entry point of our program.
- It creates a list to hold the fetch tasks and uses a loop to create multiple fetch_data tasks for different data sources.
- The asyncio.create_task() function schedules these coroutines for execution, and they are collected into a list.
- The program waits for all fetch tasks to complete using await asyncio.g ather(*fetch_tasks), which returns a list of results.
- After fetching the data, the program creates another list to hold the processing tasks, and similar to the fetching phase, it processes the fetched data concurrently.
- Finally, it waits for all processing tasks to complete.

Running the Event Loop:

- The if __name__ == "__main__": block calls asyncio.run(main()), which initializes the event loop and runs the main coroutine.

Step 3: Running the Program

To run the program, open your terminal or command prompt, navigate to the directory containing your asyncio_example.py file, and execute the following command:

```bash

python asyncio_example.py
```

As the program runs, you will see output similar to the following:

```
css
```

```
Starting to fetch data from source 0...
Starting to fetch data from source 1...
Starting to fetch data from source 2...
Starting to fetch data from source 3...
Starting to fetch data from source 4...
Completed fetching data from source 1.
Completed fetching data from source 0.
Completed fetching data from source 4.
Completed fetching data from source 3.
Completed fetching data from source 2.
Processing Data from source 0...
Processing Data from source 1...
Processing Data from source 2...
Processing Data from source 3...
Processing Data from source 4...
Finished processing Data from source 1.
Finished processing Data from source 0.
Finished processing Data from source 4.
Finished processing Data from source 3.
Finished processing Data from source 2.
```

Step 4: Observing Asynchronous Behavior

The output illustrates how the program handles multiple tasks concurrently. You'll notice that the fetching and processing of data occur simultaneously, demonstrating the power of asynchronous programming. For instance, while one task is waiting (e.g., during the await asyncio.sleep() calls), other tasks can proceed without blocking.

In this section, we have successfully written and run our first asynchronous program using Python's asyncio library. By simulating fetching and processing tasks concurrently, we have seen how to leverage coroutines and the event loop to create responsive applications.

Common Patterns in Asyncio

Asynchronous programming with asyncio allows developers to adopt various patterns that enhance code readability, maintainability, and functionality. Understanding these common patterns is essential for effectively utilizing asyncio in your applications. In this section, we will explore several common patterns and best practices in asyncio, including creating and managing tasks, handling timeouts, using synchronization primitives, and more.

1. Creating and Managing Tasks

Tasks are the building blocks of concurrency in asyncio. When you schedule a coroutine using asyncio.create_task(), it returns a Task object that wraps the coroutine. This allows the event loop to run the coroutine concurrently with other tasks.

Example of Creating Tasks:

```python
python

import asyncio

async def example_coroutine(name, delay):
    await asyncio.sleep(delay)
    print(f"{name} finished after {delay} seconds")

async def main():
    # Creating multiple tasks
    task1 = asyncio.create_task(example_coroutine("Task 1", 2))
    task2 = asyncio.create_task(example_coroutine("Task 2", 1))
    task3 = asyncio.create_task(example_coroutine("Task 3", 3))

    # Wait for all tasks to complete
    await task1
    await task2
    await task3

asyncio.run(main())
```

In this example, three tasks are created and executed concurrently. The main coroutine waits for each task to complete using await.

2. Gathering Results with asyncio.gather()

The asyncio.gather() function is a powerful tool for running multiple coroutines concurrently and collecting their results. This function accepts any number of awaitable objects (coroutines or tasks) and returns a single awaitable that resolves when all the input awaitables have completed.

Example of Using asyncio.gather():

```python
python

import asyncio

async def fetch_data(id):
    await asyncio.sleep(1)
    return f"Data {id}"

async def main():
    results = await asyncio.gather(
        fetch_data(1),
        fetch_data(2),
        fetch_data(3)
    )
    print(results)  # Output: ['Data 1', 'Data 2', 'Data 3']

asyncio.run(main())
```

This pattern is useful when you need to execute multiple asynchronous tasks and want to collect their results together.

3. Handling Timeouts

In scenarios where tasks might hang or take longer than expected, implementing timeouts is crucial for maintaining application responsiveness. The asyncio.wait_for() function allows you to set a timeout for a specific coroutine.

Example of Using asyncio.wait_for():

```python
import asyncio

async def long_running_task():
    await asyncio.sleep(5)  # Simulating a long-running task
    return "Task completed"

async def main():
    try:
        result = await asyncio.wait_for(long_running_task(),
        timeout=2)
        print(result)
    except asyncio.TimeoutError:
        print("The task timed out!")

asyncio.run(main())
```

In this example, if long_running_task does not complete within 2 seconds, a TimeoutError is raised, allowing you to handle the situation gracefully.

4. Synchronization Primitives

In asynchronous programming, synchronization is essential to ensure that shared resources are accessed safely. asyncio provides several synchronization primitives, including locks, events, and semaphores.

Example of Using an Asyncio Lock:

```python
import asyncio

lock = asyncio.Lock()

async def critical_section(name):
```

```
    async with lock:  # Acquiring the lock
        print(f"{name} entered the critical section")
        await asyncio.sleep(1)
        print(f"{name} leaving the critical section")

async def main():
    await asyncio.gather(
        critical_section("Task 1"),
        critical_section("Task 2"),
    )

asyncio.run(main())
```

In this example, the Lock ensures that only one task can enter the critical section at a time, preventing race conditions.

5. Using Events for Coordination

Events can be used to signal between coroutines. The asyncio.Event class provides a way to notify one or more coroutines that something has happened.

Example of Using asyncio.Event:

```python
import asyncio

event = asyncio.Event()

async def waiter():
    print("Waiting for the event to be set...")
    await event.wait()  # Wait until the event is set
    print("Event has been set!")

async def setter():
    await asyncio.sleep(2)
    print("Setting the event...")
    event.set()  # Set the event, allowing the waiter to proceed
```

```
async def main():
    await asyncio.gather(waiter(), setter())

asyncio.run(main())
```

In this example, the waiter coroutine waits for the setter coroutine to set the event, demonstrating how events can coordinate actions between coroutines.

6. Creating Background Tasks

Sometimes, you may want to run a coroutine as a background task while the main application continues executing. You can use asyncio.create_task() to schedule a coroutine that runs independently.

Example of Running Background Tasks:

```python

import asyncio

async def background_task():
    while True:
        print("Background task running...")
        await asyncio.sleep(1)

async def main():
    asyncio.create_task(background_task())  # Run as a background
    task
    await asyncio.sleep(5)  # Simulate main application work
    print("Main application done!")

asyncio.run(main())
```

This example shows how to run a background task that continues to execute while the main application performs other work.

7. Handling Exceptions in Asyncio

Error handling is crucial in any programming paradigm. In asyncio, you can use standard try and except blocks within coroutines to catch exceptions.

Example of Handling Exceptions:

```python
python

import asyncio

async def risky_operation():
    raise ValueError("An error occurred!")

async def main():
    try:
        await risky_operation()
    except ValueError as e:
        print(f"Caught an exception: {e}")

asyncio.run(main())
```

This example demonstrates how to catch exceptions raised by asynchronous operations, allowing you to implement robust error handling in your applications.

Understanding common patterns in asyncio is essential for developing effective asynchronous applications. By mastering these patterns—creating and managing tasks, using asyncio.gather(), handling timeouts, utilizing synchronization primitives, coordinating with events, creating background tasks, and handling exceptions—you will be well-equipped to tackle a wide range of asynchronous programming scenarios.

Making Asynchronous Network Requests

Overview of HTTP and REST APIs
   In the realm of web development and network programming, understanding the fundamentals of the Hypertext Transfer Protocol (HTTP) and Representational State Transfer (REST) APIs is crucial. This chapter provides an in-depth overview of HTTP as the foundational protocol for web communication and REST as a guiding architectural style for designing networked applications. These concepts are essential for effectively making asynchronous network requests in Python using the asyncio library.

1. Understanding HTTP

What is HTTP?

HTTP, or Hypertext Transfer Protocol, is the protocol used for transmitting data over the World Wide Web. It defines a set of rules for how messages are formatted and transmitted, as well as how web servers and browsers should respond to various requests. Developed by Tim Berners-Lee in 1989, HTTP has evolved through several versions, with HTTP/1.1 and HTTP/2 being the most widely used today.

Key Components of HTTP

- **Requests and Responses**: The communication in HTTP occurs through request-response cycles. A client (often a web browser or an application) sends an HTTP request to a server, which processes the request and returns an HTTP response.

- **Methods**: HTTP defines several request methods that specify the desired action to be performed. The most commonly used methods include:
- **GET**: Retrieves data from the server. It is used for fetching resources without modifying them.
- **POST**: Sends data to the server to create or update a resource. It typically involves submitting form data or uploading files.
- **PUT**: Updates an existing resource on the server.
- **DELETE**: Removes a resource from the server.
- **HEAD**: Similar to GET, but it retrieves only the headers, not the body of the response.
- **Status Codes**: HTTP responses include status codes that indicate the result of the request. Common status codes include:
- **200 OK**: The request was successful.
- **404 Not Found**: The requested resource was not found.
- **500 Internal Server Error**: The server encountered an unexpected condition that prevented it from fulfilling the request.
- **Headers**: HTTP messages can include headers that provide additional information about the request or response. Common headers include Content-Type, which indicates the type of data being sent (e.g., JSON, HTML), and Authorization, which is used for authentication.

HTTP/2 and Beyond

HTTP/2, which was standardized in 2015, introduced several improvements over HTTP/1.1, including:

- **Multiplexing**: Allows multiple requests and responses to be sent simultaneously over a single connection, reducing latency and improving performance.
- **Header Compression**: Reduces the size of HTTP headers, leading to faster transmission.

- **Server Push**: Enables servers to send resources to clients before they are requested, anticipating client needs.

These enhancements make HTTP/2 more efficient and suitable for modern web applications, especially those requiring real-time interactions.

2. Understanding REST APIs
What is REST?

REST, or Representational State Transfer, is an architectural style for designing networked applications. It leverages HTTP and emphasizes stateless communication, making it ideal for building scalable and interoperable web services. REST was introduced by Roy Fielding in his doctoral dissertation in 2000.

Principles of REST

REST is based on six guiding principles, which help create a clear and consistent framework for designing APIs:

Statelessness: Each request from the client to the server must contain all the information necessary to understand and process the request. The server does not store any client context between requests, leading to greater scalability.

Client-Server Architecture: REST separates the client and server concerns. The client is responsible for the user interface, while the server handles data processing and storage. This separation allows for independent evolution of the client and server.

Cacheability: Responses from the server can be marked as cacheable or non-cacheable. Caching improves performance by allowing clients to reuse previously retrieved data without making new requests.

Uniform Interface: REST APIs are designed with a uniform interface that simplifies and decouples the architecture. This principle is key to enabling the independent evolution of the client and server.

Layered System: A REST API can be composed of multiple layers, with each layer providing specific functionality (e.g., security, load balancing).

Clients cannot assume whether they are connected directly to the end server or to an intermediary.

Code on Demand (optional): Servers can extend client functionality by transferring executable code (e.g., JavaScript). This principle is optional and not commonly implemented in REST APIs.

Designing RESTful APIs

When designing RESTful APIs, certain conventions and best practices should be followed:

Resource Identification: Resources should be uniquely identifiable using URLs. For example:

- GET /users to retrieve a list of users
- POST /users to create a new user
- GET /users/1 to retrieve the user with ID 1
- PUT /users/1 to update the user with ID 1
- DELETE /users/1 to delete the user with ID 1

Use of HTTP Methods: Leverage the appropriate HTTP methods for actions:

- Use **GET** for retrieving resources.
- Use **POST** for creating resources.
- Use **PUT** for updating existing resources.
- Use **DELETE** for removing resources.

Response Format: Use standard formats such as JSON or XML for responses. JSON is the most common format due to its lightweight nature and ease of use in JavaScript.

Versioning: Implement versioning in your API to allow for changes without breaking existing clients. This can be done by including the version number in the URL (e.g., /api/v1/users).

Error Handling: Use appropriate HTTP status codes to indicate the success or failure of requests. Provide meaningful error messages in the response body to help clients understand the issue.

3. Asynchronous Requests with HTTP in Python

With a solid understanding of HTTP and REST APIs, we can now explore how to make asynchronous network requests in Python using libraries like aiohttp. This library allows you to leverage asyncio to perform non-blocking HTTP requests, enabling your applications to interact with web services efficiently.

Example of Making Asynchronous HTTP Requests

```python
import aiohttp
import asyncio

async def fetch(url):
    async with aiohttp.ClientSession() as session:
        async with session.get(url) as response:
            return await response.json()  # Assumes response is
            in JSON format

async def main():
    url = 'https://api.example.com/data'
    data = await fetch(url)
    print(data)

if __name__ == "__main__":
    asyncio.run(main())
```

In this example, we define an asynchronous fetch function that uses aiohttp to make a GET request to a specified URL. The main coroutine fetches the data and prints the JSON response.

Understanding HTTP and REST APIs is foundational for developing modern web applications and services. By mastering these concepts, you will be better equipped to build efficient, scalable, and responsive applications that interact with web services.

Using Aiohttp for Asynchronous HTTP Requests

aiohttp is a powerful library in Python designed for making asynchronous HTTP requests, built on top of the asyncio library. It provides both client and server functionality, allowing developers to create HTTP clients that can perform non-blocking network operations. In this section, we will explore how to use aiohttp for making asynchronous HTTP requests, including GET and POST requests, handling responses, managing sessions, and dealing with errors.

1. Installing Aiohttp

Before you can use aiohttp, you need to install it. If you have not done so already, you can install it using pip within your activated virtual environment:

```bash

pip install aiohttp
```

2. Making GET Requests

One of the most common use cases for aiohttp is making GET requests to retrieve data from a RESTful API. Below is an example that demonstrates how to perform a GET request and process the response.

Example of a GET Request:

```python

import aiohttp
import asyncio

async def fetch_data(url):
    async with aiohttp.ClientSession() as session:
        async with session.get(url) as response:
            # Check if the request was successful
            response.raise_for_status()  # Raises an error for
```

```
            bad responses
            return await response.json()  # Parse response as JSON

  async def main():
      url = 'https://jsonplaceholder.typicode.com/posts/1'  #
      Example API
      try:
          data = await fetch_data(url)
          print(data)
      except aiohttp.ClientError as e:
          print(f"An error occurred: {e}")

  if __name__ == "__main__":
      asyncio.run(main())
```

In this example:

- We create an asynchronous function fetch_data that takes a URL as an argument.
- Inside this function, we use aiohttp.ClientSession() to create a session. Using sessions is recommended for making multiple requests as it manages connection pooling efficiently.
- We then make a GET request to the specified URL using session.get(url).
- The response.raise_for_status() method is called to raise an exception for HTTP error responses (status codes 4xx and 5xx).
- The response body is parsed as JSON using await response.json().

3. Making POST Requests

In addition to GET requests, aiohttp allows you to make POST requests to send data to a server. Below is an example demonstrating how to send JSON data using a POST request.

Example of a POST Request:

```python
python

import aiohttp
import asyncio
import json

async def post_data(url, payload):
    async with aiohttp.ClientSession() as session:
        async with session.post(url, json=payload) as response:
            response.raise_for_status()  # Raise error for bad
            responses
            return await response.json()  # Parse response as JSON

async def main():
    url = 'https://jsonplaceholder.typicode.com/posts'  # Example
    API
    payload = {
        "title": "foo",
        "body": "bar",
        "userId": 1
    }

    try:
        response = await post_data(url, payload)
        print(response)
    except aiohttp.ClientError as e:
        print(f"An error occurred: {e}")

if __name__ == "__main__":
    asyncio.run(main())
```

In this example:

- We define an asynchronous function post_data that sends a JSON payload to the specified URL.
- The session.post(url, json=payload) method sends the JSON data directly.
- As with the GET request, we handle potential errors using response.rai se_for_status() and parse the JSON response.

51

4. Handling Multiple Requests Concurrently

One of the strengths of aiohttp is its ability to handle multiple requests concurrently. You can use asyncio.gather() to run multiple asynchronous tasks at the same time.

Example of Making Multiple Concurrent GET Requests:

```python
import aiohttp
import asyncio

async def fetch_data(url):
    async with aiohttp.ClientSession() as session:
        async with session.get(url) as response:
            response.raise_for_status()
            return await response.json()

async def main():
    urls = [
        'https://jsonplaceholder.typicode.com/posts/1',
        'https://jsonplaceholder.typicode.com/posts/2',
        'https://jsonplaceholder.typicode.com/posts/3',
    ]

    # Create a list of fetch tasks
    fetch_tasks = [fetch_data(url) for url in urls]

    try:
        results = await asyncio.gather(*fetch_tasks)
        for result in results:
            print(result)
    except aiohttp.ClientError as e:
        print(f"An error occurred: {e}")

if __name__ == "__main__":
    asyncio.run(main())
```

In this example:

- We define a list of URLs to fetch data from.
- We create a list of fetch tasks using a list comprehension.
- We use asyncio.gather() to run all the fetch tasks concurrently and collect the results.

5. Error Handling in Aiohttp

Handling errors is crucial when making network requests. aiohttp provides a variety of exceptions to help manage different error scenarios. Here's a summary of some common exceptions:

- **aiohttp.ClientError**: The base class for all client-related errors.
- **aiohttp.HTTPError**: Raised for HTTP errors (4xx and 5xx responses).
- **aiohttp.Timeout**: Raised when a request exceeds the specified timeout.

Example of Handling Different Errors:

```python
import aiohttp
import asyncio

async def fetch_data(url):
    async with aiohttp.ClientSession() as session:
        try:
            async with session.get(url) as response:
                response.raise_for_status()  # Raise error for
                bad responses
                return await response.json()
        except aiohttp.ClientError as e:
            print(f"Client error: {e}")
        except aiohttp.Timeout:
            print("Request timed out")

async def main():
    url = 'https://jsonplaceholder.typicode.com/posts/1'
    await fetch_data(url)
```

```
if __name__ == "__main__":
    asyncio.run(main())
```

In this example, we handle ClientError and Timeout separately, allowing for more granular error management.

6. Managing Sessions

Using sessions effectively is vital for managing connections and improving performance in aiohttp. A session maintains connections across requests, allowing for efficient reuse.

- Always create a single session for multiple requests when possible to take advantage of connection pooling.
- Use the session context manager to ensure proper cleanup after requests.

Example of Using a Session in a Context Manager:

```python
python

import aiohttp
import asyncio

async def fetch_data(url, session):
    async with session.get(url) as response:
        response.raise_for_status()
        return await response.json()

async def main():
    urls = [
        'https://jsonplaceholder.typicode.com/posts/1',
        'https://jsonplaceholder.typicode.com/posts/2',
    ]
```

```
async with aiohttp.ClientSession() as session:  # Context
manager for session
    fetch_tasks = [fetch_data(url, session) for url in urls]
    results = await asyncio.gather(*fetch_tasks)
    print(results)

if __name__ == "__main__":
    asyncio.run(main())
```

In this example, we pass the session to each fetch_data call, ensuring efficient connection reuse.

Using aiohttp for asynchronous HTTP requests allows developers to build efficient, responsive applications that interact seamlessly with web services. By understanding how to perform GET and POST requests, handle multiple requests concurrently, manage sessions, and deal with errors, you can effectively leverage the power of asyncio to enhance your network programming capabilities.

Handling JSON Data in Asynchronous Contexts

JSON (JavaScript Object Notation) is a widely used format for data interchange, particularly in web applications. When working with asynchronous requests in Python using the aiohttp library, handling JSON data efficiently is crucial for creating responsive applications that interact with APIs. This section explores how to work with JSON data in asynchronous contexts, including parsing, serializing, and managing complex data structures.

1. What is JSON?

JSON is a lightweight data interchange format that is easy for humans to read and write and easy for machines to parse and generate. It is language-agnostic and is commonly used for representing structured data in a simple text format. JSON supports basic data types, including:

- **Objects**: Collections of key-value pairs enclosed in curly braces {}.
- **Arrays**: Ordered lists of values enclosed in square brackets [].
- **Strings**: Text data enclosed in double quotes.
- **Numbers**: Numeric values (both integers and floating-point).
- **Booleans**: true and false.
- **Null**: Represents a null value (null).

Example of JSON Data:

```json
json

{
    "userId": 1,
    "id": 1,
    "title": "Sample Title",
    "completed": false,
    "tags": ["example", "test"],
    "details": {
        "description": "This is a sample JSON object."
    }
}
```

2. Parsing JSON Data from HTTP Responses

When making asynchronous requests using aiohttp, it is common to receive JSON responses from APIs. You can easily parse JSON data using the response.json() method, which converts the JSON content into a Python dictionary.

Example of Parsing JSON from an Asynchronous Response:

```python
python

import aiohttp
import asyncio

async def fetch_data(url):
```

```
    async with aiohttp.ClientSession() as session:
        async with session.get(url) as response:
            response.raise_for_status()  # Check for HTTP errors
            json_data = await response.json()  # Parse JSON
            response
            return json_data

async def main():
    url = 'https://jsonplaceholder.typicode.com/todos/1'
    data = await fetch_data(url)
    print(data)

if __name__ == "__main__":
    asyncio.run(main())
```

In this example:

- We make a GET request to a sample API endpoint.
- We call await response.json() to parse the response body into a Python dictionary.

3. Serializing Python Objects to JSON

In addition to parsing JSON data, you may need to send JSON data in requests (e.g., during a POST operation). You can serialize Python dictionaries and lists into JSON format using the json module from the standard library.

Example of Serializing Data to JSON:

```
python

import aiohttp
import asyncio
import json

async def post_data(url, payload):
```

```
    async with aiohttp.ClientSession() as session:
        async with session.post(url, json=payload) as response:
            response.raise_for_status()
            return await response.json()

async def main():
    url = 'https://jsonplaceholder.typicode.com/posts'
    payload = {
        "title": "foo",
        "body": "bar",
        "userId": 1
    }

    response = await post_data(url, payload)
    print(response)

if __name__ == "__main__":
    asyncio.run(main())
```

In this example:

- The post_data function takes a payload dictionary and sends it as JSON using session.post(url, json=payload).
- The json parameter automatically handles serialization, ensuring that the data is properly formatted.

4. Working with Nested JSON Structures

When dealing with APIs, you often encounter nested JSON structures. Accessing and manipulating these structures in Python requires understanding how to traverse dictionaries and lists.

Example of Accessing Nested JSON Data:

```python
python

import aiohttp
import asyncio
```

```python
async def fetch_data(url):
    async with aiohttp.ClientSession() as session:
        async with session.get(url) as response:
            response.raise_for_status()
            return await response.json()

async def main():
    url = 'https://jsonplaceholder.typicode.com/todos/1'
    data = await fetch_data(url)

    # Accessing nested data
    user_id = data['userId']
    title = data['title']
    completed = data['completed']

    print(f"User ID: {user_id}, Title: {title}, Completed:
    {completed}")

if __name__ == "__main__":
    asyncio.run(main())
```

In this example:

- We fetch a TODO item and access nested values using dictionary keys.
- You can access nested objects by chaining the keys, like data['details']['description'] if the structure permits.

5. Handling JSON Serialization Errors

When serializing data to JSON, it's important to handle potential errors, particularly when working with non-serializable Python objects (e.g., custom classes, sets). You can use json.dumps() to explicitly serialize objects and handle exceptions.

Example of Handling Serialization Errors:

```python
python

import aiohttp
import asyncio
import json

class CustomObject:
    def __init__(self, name):
        self.name = name

async def post_data(url, payload):
    async with aiohttp.ClientSession() as session:
        async with session.post(url, json=payload) as response:
            response.raise_for_status()
            return await response.json()

async def main():
    url = 'https://jsonplaceholder.typicode.com/posts'
    payload = {
        "title": "foo",
        "body": "bar",
        "userId": 1,
        "custom": CustomObject("example")
    }

    try:
        # Attempt to serialize the payload
        json_payload = json.dumps(payload)  # This will raise an
        error
        response = await post_data(url, json_payload)
        print(response)
    except TypeError as e:
        print(f"Serialization error: {e}")

if __name__ == "__main__":
    asyncio.run(main())
```

In this example:

- We attempt to serialize a payload that includes a custom object.

- The json.dumps() function raises a TypeError, which we catch and handle gracefully.

6. Validating JSON Responses

When working with JSON responses from APIs, it's crucial to validate the data to ensure it meets your application's requirements. You can implement simple validation checks or use libraries like jsonschema to enforce more complex validation rules.

Example of Simple Validation:

```python
import aiohttp
import asyncio

async def fetch_data(url):
    async with aiohttp.ClientSession() as session:
        async with session.get(url) as response:
            response.raise_for_status()
            return await response.json()

async def main():
    url = 'https://jsonplaceholder.typicode.com/todos/1'
    data = await fetch_data(url)

    # Validate the response structure
    if all(key in data for key in ['userId', 'id', 'title',
    'completed']):
        print("Response is valid.")
        print(data)
    else:
        print("Invalid response structure.")

if __name__ == "__main__":
    asyncio.run(main())
```

In this example:

- We validate that the response contains the expected keys before proceeding to process the data.

Handling JSON data in asynchronous contexts is a vital skill for developers working with APIs and web services. By effectively parsing and serializing JSON, accessing nested structures, handling errors, and validating responses, you can build robust applications that interact seamlessly with various data sources.

Managing Connections and Sessions

Efficient management of connections and sessions is critical when developing applications that make asynchronous HTTP requests using the aiohttp library. By properly managing connections, you can improve performance, reduce latency, and ensure resource efficiency in your applications. This section explores how to effectively manage connections and sessions in aiohttp, including the use of connection pooling, session lifecycle management, and best practices for optimal performance.

1. Understanding Client Sessions

A client session in aiohttp is a context manager that manages connections for your HTTP requests. Using a session allows you to maintain persistent connections, which can significantly improve the performance of your application, especially when making multiple requests to the same server. Sessions handle connection pooling and reuse underlying connections, reducing the overhead associated with establishing new connections for every request.

Creating a Client Session

You can create a client session using the aiohttp.ClientSession() class. It is best practice to create a session once and reuse it for multiple requests rather than creating a new session for each request.

Example of Creating and Using a Client Session:

```python
python

import aiohttp
import asyncio

async def fetch_data(url, session):
    async with session.get(url) as response:
        response.raise_for_status()  # Check for HTTP errors
        return await response.json()  # Parse JSON response

async def main():
    url = 'https://jsonplaceholder.typicode.com/posts/1'
    async with aiohttp.ClientSession() as session:  # Context
    manager for session
        data = await fetch_data(url, session)
        print(data)

if __name__ == "__main__":
    asyncio.run(main())
```

In this example, we create a client session using a context manager, ensuring that the session is properly closed after its use.

2. Connection Pooling

Connection pooling is a technique used to manage and reuse connections, improving performance by minimizing the overhead associated with creating new connections. aiohttp automatically implements connection pooling when you use a ClientSession.

How Connection Pooling Works

When a session is created, it maintains a pool of connections to the server. When a request is made, aiohttp will check if an existing connection can be reused. If an appropriate connection is available, it will be used; otherwise, a new connection will be established.

This pooling mechanism is particularly useful when making multiple requests to the same server, as it reduces the time spent in the connection setup phase.

Example of Connection Pooling:

```python
python

import aiohttp
import asyncio

async def fetch_data(url, session):
    async with session.get(url) as response:
        response.raise_for_status()
        return await response.json()

async def main():
    urls = [
        'https://jsonplaceholder.typicode.com/posts/1',
        'https://jsonplaceholder.typicode.com/posts/2',
        'https://jsonplaceholder.typicode.com/posts/3',
    ]

    async with aiohttp.ClientSession() as session:
        fetch_tasks = [fetch_data(url, session) for url in urls]
        results = await asyncio.gather(*fetch_tasks)
        print(results)

if __name__ == "__main__":
    asyncio.run(main())
```

In this example, multiple GET requests are made using the same session. The connection pool allows efficient reuse of connections, resulting in faster execution times.

3. Session Lifecycle Management

Managing the lifecycle of client sessions is essential for preventing resource leaks and ensuring optimal performance. You should create a session at the start of your application and close it once all requests are complete.

Closing the Session

Using a session as a context manager automatically handles closing the session when it is no longer needed. However, if you create a session outside of a context manager, you must explicitly close it to release resources.

Example of Closing a Session Explicitly:

python

```
import aiohttp
import asyncio

async def fetch_data(url, session):
    async with session.get(url) as response:
        response.raise_for_status()
        return await response.json()

async def main():
    url = 'https://jsonplaceholder.typicode.com/posts/1'
    session = aiohttp.ClientSession()  # Create a session outside
    of a context manager
    try:
        data = await fetch_data(url, session)
        print(data)
    finally:
        await session.close()  # Explicitly close the session

if __name__ == "__main__":
    asyncio.run(main())
```

In this example, we create a session and ensure it is closed in the finally block, which guarantees that resources are released even if an error occurs.

4. Customizing Client Sessions

aiohttp.ClientSession can be customized to meet the specific needs of your application. You can configure parameters such as timeout settings, headers, authentication, and more.

Setting Timeouts

You can set timeouts for your requests to avoid waiting indefinitely for a response. The timeout parameter can be set when creating a session.

Example of Setting a Timeout:

```python
import aiohttp
import asyncio

async def fetch_data(url, session):
    async with session.get(url) as response:
        response.raise_for_status()
        return await response.json()

async def main():
    timeout = aiohttp.ClientTimeout(total=5)  # Set a total
    timeout of 5 seconds
    async with aiohttp.ClientSession(timeout=timeout) as session:
        url = 'https://jsonplaceholder.typicode.com/posts/1'
        data = await fetch_data(url, session)
        print(data)

if __name__ == "__main__":
    asyncio.run(main())
```

In this example, we create a ClientTimeout instance to specify a total timeout for all requests made using that session.

Adding Custom Headers

You can add custom headers to your requests to include authentication tokens, content types, or other relevant information.

Example of Adding Custom Headers:

```python
import aiohttp
import asyncio
```

```python
async def fetch_data(url, session):
    async with session.get(url) as response:
        response.raise_for_status()
        return await response.json()

async def main():
    headers = {
        'Authorization': 'Bearer YOUR_API_TOKEN',
        'Content-Type': 'application/json',
    }

    async with aiohttp.ClientSession() as session:
        url = 'https://jsonplaceholder.typicode.com/posts/1'
        data = await fetch_data(url, session)
        print(data)

if __name__ == "__main__":
    asyncio.run(main())
```

In this example, we define a dictionary of headers to be included in the request. You can pass these headers to the session.get() or session.post() methods as an additional parameter.

5. Best Practices for Managing Connections and Sessions

To ensure optimal performance and resource management in your aiohttp applications, consider the following best practices:

1. **Use a Single Session**: Create a single instance of ClientSession and reuse it for multiple requests instead of creating a new session for each request.
2. **Close Sessions Properly**: Always ensure that sessions are closed when no longer needed. Use context managers where possible to simplify session lifecycle management.
3. **Leverage Connection Pooling**: Take advantage of connection pooling by reusing sessions, which reduces connection establishment overhead and improves request latency.

4. **Handle Timeouts**: Set appropriate timeout values to prevent long waits for unresponsive servers and handle scenarios where requests might hang.

5. **Use Custom Headers**: When making API requests, include any necessary custom headers for authentication or content type to ensure your requests are processed correctly.

6. **Monitor Resource Usage**: Keep an eye on the resource usage of your application, particularly when dealing with high volumes of requests. This helps in identifying bottlenecks and optimizing performance.

Effective management of connections and sessions is fundamental to building efficient asynchronous applications using the aiohttp library. By leveraging client sessions, connection pooling, session lifecycle management, and best practices, you can enhance the performance and reliability of your applications.

Error Handling in Asynchronous HTTP Requests

Effective error handling is essential when making asynchronous HTTP requests using the aiohttp library. Network operations are inherently unreliable, and your application should gracefully handle various error scenarios to ensure a robust user experience. This section explores common error types in asynchronous HTTP requests, strategies for handling them, and best practices for implementing error management in your applications.

1. Common Error Types

When working with aiohttp, several types of errors may arise during HTTP requests:

- **Network Errors**: Issues related to connectivity, such as DNS resolution failures or connection timeouts, can occur. These errors may prevent the client from reaching the server.

- **HTTP Errors**: The server may respond with HTTP status codes that indicate errors, such as:
- **4xx Client Errors**: Errors indicating issues with the request (e.g., 404 Not Found, 401 Unauthorized).
- **5xx Server Errors**: Errors indicating problems on the server side (e.g., 500 Internal Server Error).
- **Timeout Errors**: Requests may take too long to complete, leading to a timeout. This can happen if the server is slow to respond or if network latency is high.
- **Invalid Response Errors**: The response received may not be in the expected format (e.g., non-JSON responses when JSON is expected).

2. Handling Errors with aiohttp

To manage errors effectively in aiohttp, you can use try and except blocks around your request calls. This allows you to catch specific exceptions and implement appropriate error handling logic.

Example of Basic Error Handling:

python

```python
import aiohttp
import asyncio

async def fetch_data(url):
    async with aiohttp.ClientSession() as session:
        try:
            async with session.get(url) as response:
                response.raise_for_status()  # Raise for HTTP
                errors
                return await response.json()  # Parse JSON
                response
        except aiohttp.ClientError as e:
            print(f"Client error: {e}")
        except aiohttp.HTTPError as e:
            print(f"HTTP error: {e}")
        except asyncio.TimeoutError:
```

```python
            print("Request timed out.")
        except Exception as e:
            print(f"An unexpected error occurred: {e}")

async def main():
    url = 'https://jsonplaceholder.typicode.com/posts/1'
    data = await fetch_data(url)
    if data:
        print(data)

if __name__ == "__main__":
    asyncio.run(main())
```

In this example:

- We catch aiohttp.ClientError for general client-related issues.
- We specifically handle aiohttp.HTTPError for HTTP response errors.
- We catch asyncio.TimeoutError for requests that exceed their time limits.
- A generic exception handler is included to catch any other unexpected errors.

3. Customizing Error Messages

When handling errors, providing informative messages can help users or developers understand what went wrong. You can enhance error handling by customizing the messages based on the type of error encountered.

Example of Customized Error Handling:

```python
python

import aiohttp
import asyncio

async def fetch_data(url):
    async with aiohttp.ClientSession() as session:
```

```
        try:
            async with session.get(url) as response:
                response.raise_for_status()
                return await response.json()
        except aiohttp.ClientError as e:
            print(f"Error while fetching data: {e}")
        except aiohttp.HTTPError as e:
            print(f"HTTP error {response.status}:
            {response.reason} for URL: {url}")
        except asyncio.TimeoutError:
            print(f"Request to {url} timed out.")
        except Exception as e:
            print(f"An unexpected error occurred: {e}")

async def main():
    url = 'https://jsonplaceholder.typicode.com/posts/100'  #
    Example of a non-existent resource
    data = await fetch_data(url)
    if data:
        print(data)

if __name__ == "__main__":
    asyncio.run(main())
```

In this enhanced example:

- We include the HTTP status code and reason in the error message for HTTP errors, making it clear what went wrong and which URL was involved.

4. Implementing Retry Logic

In cases where errors are transient (e.g., temporary network issues), implementing a retry mechanism can improve the resilience of your application. You can use a simple loop to retry the request a specified number of times before giving up.

Example of Simple Retry Logic:

```python
python

import aiohttp
import asyncio

async def fetch_data(url, retries=3):
    async with aiohttp.ClientSession() as session:
        for attempt in range(retries):
            try:
                async with session.get(url) as response:
                    response.raise_for_status()  # Raise for HTTP
                    errors
                    return await response.json()
            except aiohttp.ClientError as e:
                print(f"Attempt {attempt + 1}: Client error -
                {e}")
            except aiohttp.HTTPError as e:
                print(f"Attempt {attempt + 1}: HTTP error - {e}")
            except asyncio.TimeoutError:
                print(f"Attempt {attempt + 1}: Request timed
                out.")
            await asyncio.sleep(1)  # Wait before retrying

        print("All attempts failed.")
        return None

async def main():
    url = 'https://jsonplaceholder.typicode.com/posts/1'
    data = await fetch_data(url)
    if data:
        print(data)

if __name__ == "__main__":
    asyncio.run(main())
```

In this example:

- The fetch_data function attempts to fetch the data up to retries times.
- After each failed attempt, it waits for 1 second before retrying, allowing

for transient issues to resolve.

5. Logging Errors for Debugging

In production applications, logging errors is crucial for monitoring and debugging. Instead of printing errors to the console, consider using the built-in logging module to log errors with varying severity levels.

Example of Using the Logging Module:

python

```python
import aiohttp
import asyncio
import logging

logging.basicConfig(level=logging.ERROR)  # Configure logging
level

async def fetch_data(url):
    async with aiohttp.ClientSession() as session:
        try:
            async with session.get(url) as response:
                response.raise_for_status()
                return await response.json()
        except aiohttp.ClientError as e:
            logging.error(f"Client error: {e}")
        except aiohttp.HTTPError as e:
            logging.error(f"HTTP error {response.status}:
            {response.reason} for URL: {url}")
        except asyncio.TimeoutError:
            logging.error(f"Request to {url} timed out.")
        except Exception as e:
            logging.error(f"An unexpected error occurred: {e}")

async def main():
    url = 'https://jsonplaceholder.typicode.com/posts/100'  #
    Example of a non-existent resource
    data = await fetch_data(url)
    if data:
```

```
        print(data)

if __name__ == "__main__":
    asyncio.run(main())
```

In this example:

- We configure logging to display error messages.
- Instead of using print, we log errors using logging.error(), which provides a standardized way to handle error messages in applications.

Error handling is a vital aspect of developing robust asynchronous applications using aiohttp. By understanding the common types of errors, implementing effective handling strategies, customizing error messages, adding retry logic, and leveraging logging, you can create applications that are resilient to network failures and provide a better user experience.

Building a Simple Asynchronous Chat Application

O verview of the Chat Application Architecture
    In this chapter, we will explore the architecture of a simple asynchronous chat application built using Python's asyncio and aiohttp libraries. Chat applications are excellent examples of real-time applications that benefit from asynchronous programming, as they need to handle multiple concurrent connections, deliver messages instantly, and maintain responsiveness. Understanding the architecture will provide a solid foundation for building a functional and efficient chat application.

Core Components of the Chat Application

The architecture of a chat application typically consists of several key components that work together to facilitate real-time communication between users. Below are the primary components we will discuss:

Client: The client represents the user interface where users interact with the chat application. It sends messages to the server and displays messages received from other users.

WebSocket Server: The server manages communication between connected clients. It receives messages from one client and broadcasts them to all other connected clients, ensuring real-time message delivery.

Message Handling: The server processes incoming messages, validates them, and determines how to route them to other clients. This component ensures that messages are delivered accurately and promptly.

Session Management: The server tracks connected clients, maintaining their session information (e.g., user IDs, connection status). This component is essential for managing user presence and message routing.

Frontend Interface: The frontend is the user interface of the chat application, built using web technologies (HTML, CSS, and JavaScript). It allows users to send and receive messages and displays chat history.

Backend Logic: The backend encompasses the server-side logic that handles WebSocket connections, processes messages, and manages user sessions. This logic is implemented using asynchronous programming techniques to ensure responsiveness.

Architecture Diagram

To visualize the architecture, we can represent the chat application components and their interactions in a simplified architecture diagram:

```lua
```

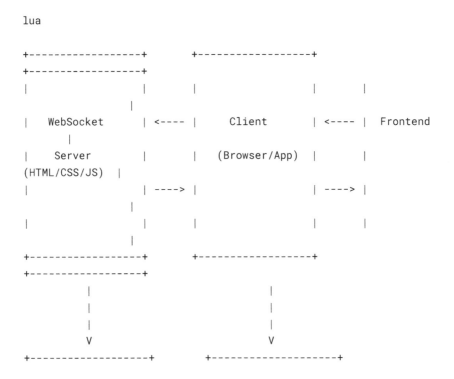

```
|                  |       |                    |
|  Message Handler | <----->|  Session Manager  |
|                  |       |                    |
+------------------+       +--------------------+
```

Detailed Component Descriptions

Let's explore each component in more detail to understand its role within the chat application architecture.

Client

The client is the primary interface through which users interact with the chat application. In our chat application, the client will be implemented as a web application that uses HTML for structure, CSS for styling, and JavaScript for functionality.

- **User Input**: Users will input messages using a text field and submit them via a button.
- **Displaying Messages**: The client will display incoming messages in a chat window, allowing users to see the conversation in real-time.
- **WebSocket Connection**: The client establishes a WebSocket connection to the server, enabling full-duplex communication for sending and receiving messages without requiring constant HTTP requests.

WebSocket Server

The WebSocket server is responsible for managing real-time communication between clients. Unlike traditional HTTP, which is request-response-based, WebSockets enable persistent connections that allow for instant message delivery.

- **Connection Management**: The server will handle incoming WebSocket connections, keeping track of each connected client. When a user connects, their session is created and added to the server's client list.
- **Message Broadcasting**: When the server receives a message from one

client, it broadcasts that message to all other connected clients. This ensures that all users receive real-time updates.

- **Asynchronous Processing**: The server uses asynchronous programming to handle multiple connections simultaneously without blocking, allowing for a responsive chat experience.

Message Handling

The message handling component is crucial for processing the flow of messages between clients. It is responsible for:

- **Receiving Messages**: The server listens for incoming messages from connected clients.
- **Validating Messages**: Incoming messages can be validated to ensure they meet specific criteria (e.g., non-empty messages).
- **Broadcasting Messages**: After processing, the server broadcasts the message to all connected clients, updating their interfaces in real time.

Session Management

Session management is essential for maintaining the state of connected clients. This component will handle:

- **Tracking Users**: The server keeps track of connected users, their session identifiers, and connection statuses.
- **User Presence**: It can manage user presence in the chat, allowing other clients to see who is online or offline.
- **Connection Cleanup**: When a user disconnects, the server should clean up their session information to avoid memory leaks.

Frontend Interface

The frontend interface is the visual representation of the chat application that users interact with. It is responsible for:

- **User Interface**: Providing a clean and intuitive layout for users to send and view messages.

- **Real-Time Updates**: Updating the chat window dynamically as messages are received, ensuring that users see conversations in real time.
- **Styling and UX**: Implementing responsive design principles to ensure the chat application is usable on various devices, including desktops and mobile phones.

Backend Logic

The backend logic encapsulates all the server-side operations that enable the chat application's functionality. This includes:

- **WebSocket Integration**: Setting up the WebSocket server to accept connections and handle communication between clients.
- **Handling Events**: Managing events related to user connections, disconnections, and message reception.
- **Error Handling**: Implementing mechanisms to gracefully handle errors, such as connection issues or unexpected message formats.

Technologies Used

To build the asynchronous chat application, we will utilize the following technologies:

- **Python**: The programming language used to implement the server-side logic.
- **aiohttp**: A library for creating the asynchronous WebSocket server and handling HTTP requests.
- **HTML/CSS/JavaScript**: The technologies used to create the client-side interface.
- **WebSockets**: A protocol that enables real-time, full-duplex communication between clients and the server.

Understanding the architecture of the chat application is a critical step toward building a functional and responsive system. By examining the core components—clients, WebSocket server, message handling, session management, frontend interface, and backend logic—we can see how they work together to facilitate real-time communication.

Setting Up the Project Environment

Setting up the project environment is a critical step in developing an asynchronous chat application using Python's asyncio and aiohttp libraries. A well-organized environment ensures that dependencies are managed effectively and that the development process runs smoothly. In this section, we will go through the steps needed to create a clean project structure, install required dependencies, and prepare for development.

1. Creating a Project Directory

Start by creating a dedicated directory for your chat application project. This directory will contain all your source code, configuration files, and any necessary assets.

Steps to Create a Project Directory:

Open your terminal or command prompt.
Navigate to the location where you want to create your project.
Create a new directory for your project, for example, async_chat_app.

bash

```
mkdir async_chat_app
cd async_chat_app
```

2. Setting Up a Virtual Environment

To isolate your project's dependencies from the system Python environment, it's best practice to create a virtual environment. This allows you to manage dependencies without affecting other projects or the global Python installation.

Steps to Create a Virtual Environment:

Create a virtual environment using Python's built-in venv module:

bash

```
python -m venv venv
```

Activate the virtual environment:

- **Windows**:

bash

```
venv\Scripts\activate
```

- **macOS and Linux**:

bash

```
source venv/bin/activate
```

Once activated, your terminal prompt should change to indicate that you are working within the virtual environment.

3. Installing Required Dependencies

With the virtual environment set up and activated, the next step is to install the necessary libraries for building the chat application. For this project, we will primarily need aiohttp for handling WebSocket connections and HTTP requests.

Steps to Install Dependencies:

Install aiohttp using pip:

```bash
bash

pip install aiohttp
```

Optionally, install aiohttp's development server capabilities (if needed):

```bash
bash

pip install aiohttp[dev]
```

Verify that aiohttp has been installed correctly:

```bash
bash

pip list
```

This command should display aiohttp in the list of installed packages.

4. Creating the Project Structure

Next, you will want to set up a clear project structure that organizes your files logically. A recommended structure for our chat application might look like this:

```
graphql

async_chat_app/ │ ├──

    venv/                    # Virtual environment │ ├──

    app.py                   # Main application file │ ├──
```

```
static/                     # Directory for static files (CSS,
JS) |  ├───────
    styles.css          # CSS styles |   └───────
    script.js           # JavaScript for client-side
    functionality |  ├──────

templates/                  # Directory for HTML
templates |   └───────
    index.html          # Main HTML file for the chat
    interface |   └───────

README.md                   # Project documentation
```

Steps to Create the Project Structure:
Create the directories and files:

```
bash
```

```bash
mkdir static templates
touch app.py templates/index.html static/styles.css
static/script.js README.md
```

Open the README.md file and provide a brief overview of your project, including setup instructions and features.

5. Initializing the HTML Template
In templates/index.html, you can set up the basic HTML structure for your chat application's user interface. Here's a simple example to get you started:

```
html
```

```html
<!DOCTYPE html>
<html lang="en">
<head>
```

```html
    <meta charset="UTF-8">
    <meta name="viewport" content="width=device-width,
    initial-scale=1.0">
    <title>Async Chat Application</title>
    <link rel="stylesheet" href="styles.css">
</head>
<body>
    <div id="chat-container">
        <h1>Chat Application</h1>
        <div id="messages"></div>
        <input type="text" id="message-input" placeholder="Type a
        message..." autocomplete="off">
        <button id="send-button">Send</button>
    </div>
    <script src="script.js"></script>
</body>
</html>
```

This HTML structure includes a chat container with a message display area, an input field for typing messages, and a send button.

6. Setting Up the JavaScript File

In static/script.js, you will implement the JavaScript needed to handle user interactions and communicate with the server via WebSockets.

Example of Basic JavaScript for WebSocket Communication:

```javascript
javascript

const messageInput = document.getElementById('message-input');
const sendButton = document.getElementById('send-button');
const messagesContainer = document.getElementById('messages');

// Create a WebSocket connection
const socket = new WebSocket('ws://localhost:8080/ws'); // Adjust
the URL based on your server configuration

socket.onmessage = function(event) {
```

```
    const message = JSON.parse(event.data);
    const messageElement = document.createElement('div');
    messageElement.textContent = message.content; // Assuming
    'content' holds the message text
    messagesContainer.appendChild(messageElement);
};


// Send message on button click
sendButton.onclick = function() {
    const message = messageInput.value;
    if (message) {
        socket.send(JSON.stringify({ content: message }));
        messageInput.value = ''; // Clear the input field
    }
};
```

In this JavaScript code:

- We establish a WebSocket connection to the server.
- We listen for incoming messages and append them to the messages container.
- We send messages typed into the input field when the send button is clicked.

In this section, we have set up the project environment for building a simple asynchronous chat application using aiohttp. By creating a structured project directory, setting up a virtual environment, installing dependencies, and initializing the HTML and JavaScript files, you are now prepared to dive into the implementation of the WebSocket server and the core functionalities of your chat application.

Creating the Server with Asyncio

In this section, we will develop the WebSocket server for our asynchronous chat application using Python's asyncio and aiohttp libraries.

This server will handle client connections, manage incoming messages, and facilitate real-time communication between users. By leveraging asynchronous programming, the server will be able to efficiently handle multiple connections concurrently, ensuring a responsive chat experience.

1. Setting Up the WebSocket Server

The WebSocket server will listen for incoming WebSocket connections and manage message exchanges between clients. Below are the steps to create the server.

Importing Required Libraries

First, you will need to import the necessary modules in your app.py file.

```python
import asyncio
import aiohttp
from aiohttp import web
```

Creating the WebSocket Handler

Next, you will define a WebSocket handler function that manages connections and message exchanges.

Example of a WebSocket Handler:

```python
clients = set()  # Set to keep track of connected clients

async def websocket_handler(request):
    ws = web.WebSocketResponse()  # Create a WebSocket response
    await ws.prepare(request)  # Prepare the WebSocket connection
    clients.add(ws)  # Add the client to the set of connected
    clients

    try:
        async for msg in ws:  # Listen for incoming messages
            if msg.type == web.WSMsgType.TEXT:
```

```
                # Broadcast the message to all connected clients
                for client in clients:
                    if client is not ws:  # Don't send the
                    message back to the sender
                        await client.send_str(msg.data)
            elif msg.type == web.WSMsgType.ERROR:
                print(f'WebSocket error: {ws.exception()}')
    finally:
        clients.remove(ws)  # Remove the client when disconnected
        await ws.close()  # Close the WebSocket connection

    return ws
```

In this handler:

- We create a WebSocketResponse object and prepare it for incoming connections.
- The client is added to a set of connected clients.
- We listen for incoming messages using an asynchronous loop (async for).
- When a message is received, it is broadcast to all other connected clients.
- The client is removed from the set of connected clients when they disconnect.

Creating the Application and Adding Routes

After defining the WebSocket handler, you need to set up the web application and define the routes.

Example of Setting Up the Application:

```python
async def init_app():
    app = web.Application()  # Create a new web application
    app.router.add_get('/ws', websocket_handler)  # Define a
    route for WebSocket connections
```

```python
    return app
```

In this function, we create an instance of web.Application() and add a route that points to the WebSocket handler.

Running the Server

Finally, you need to run the server and start listening for incoming connections. Add the following code to your app.py file:

python

```python
if __name__ == '__main__':
    app = asyncio.run(init_app())  # Initialize the application
    web.run_app(app, host='localhost', port=8080)  # Run the app
    on the specified host and port
```

In this section, we:

- Initialize the application with asyncio.run(init_app()).
- Start the web server using web.run_app(app, host='localhost', port=8080), which listens for incoming connections on localhost at port 8080.

2. Complete Code for the Server

Here's the complete app.py code for the WebSocket server:

python

```python
import asyncio
import aiohttp
from aiohttp import web

clients = set()  # Set to keep track of connected clients

async def websocket_handler(request):
```

```
    ws = web.WebSocketResponse()  # Create a WebSocket response
    await ws.prepare(request)  # Prepare the WebSocket connection
    clients.add(ws)  # Add the client to the set of connected
    clients

    try:
        async for msg in ws:  # Listen for incoming messages
            if msg.type == web.WSMsgType.TEXT:
                # Broadcast the message to all connected clients
                for client in clients:
                    if client is not ws:  # Don't send the
                    message back to the sender
                        await client.send_str(msg.data)
            elif msg.type == web.WSMsgType.ERROR:
                print(f'WebSocket error: {ws.exception()}')
    finally:
        clients.remove(ws)  # Remove the client when disconnected
        await ws.close()  # Close the WebSocket connection

    return ws

async def init_app():
    app = web.Application()  # Create a new web application
    app.router.add_get('/ws', websocket_handler)  # Define a
    route for WebSocket connections
    return app

if __name__ == '__main__':
    app = asyncio.run(init_app())  # Initialize the application
    web.run_app(app, host='localhost', port=8080)  # Run the app
    on the specified host and port
```

3. Testing the WebSocket Server

To test your WebSocket server, you can use a web client (the frontend interface created in a previous section) to establish a connection and send messages. Make sure your server is running by executing the app.py script.

Open your terminal and run the server:

```bash

python app.py
```

Open your web browser and navigate to the frontend of your chat application (ensure the HTML file is being served, or use a simple static server).

Use the chat interface to send messages. You should see the messages broadcasted to all connected clients in real time.

In this section, we have successfully set up a WebSocket server for our asynchronous chat application using asyncio and aiohttp. By implementing a WebSocket handler, managing client connections, and broadcasting messages, we laid the groundwork for real-time communication between users.

Implementing the Client-Side Logic

With the WebSocket server set up and functioning, the next step is to implement the client-side logic of the asynchronous chat application. This logic will facilitate user interactions, handle sending and receiving messages, and update the user interface in real time. In this section, we will focus on creating the JavaScript functionality needed to interact with the WebSocket server and enhance the chat application's user experience.

1. Setting Up the HTML Structure

Before diving into the JavaScript logic, ensure that you have a basic HTML structure in place. We will be working with the index.html file located in the templates directory.

Here's a refresher on the structure of index.html:

```html

```

```
<!DOCTYPE html>
<html lang="en">
<head>
    <meta charset="UTF-8">
    <meta name="viewport" content="width=device-width,
    initial-scale=1.0">
    <title>Async Chat Application</title>
    <link rel="stylesheet" href="styles.css">
</head>
<body>
    <div id="chat-container">
        <h1>Chat Application</h1>
        <div id="messages"></div>
        <input type="text" id="message-input" placeholder="Type a
        message..." autocomplete="off">
        <button id="send-button">Send</button>
    </div>
    <script src="script.js"></script>
</body>
</html>
```

Ensure that the script.js file is linked at the bottom of the HTML document to allow the DOM to load before the script runs.

2. Establishing the WebSocket Connection

In your static/script.js file, the first step is to create a WebSocket connection to the server. This will enable real-time communication between the client and the server.

Example of Establishing a WebSocket Connection:

```javascript

const messageInput = document.getElementById('message-input');
const sendButton = document.getElementById('send-button');
const messagesContainer = document.getElementById('messages');

// Create a WebSocket connection
```

```
const socket = new WebSocket('ws://localhost:8080/ws'); // Adjust
the URL as necessary

// Handle incoming messages
socket.onmessage = function(event) {
    const message = JSON.parse(event.data); // Parse the incoming
    JSON message
    const messageElement = document.createElement('div');
    messageElement.textContent = message.content; // Assuming
    'content' holds the message text
    messagesContainer.appendChild(messageElement); // Append the
    message to the chat window
};

// Handle connection open event
socket.onopen = function() {
    console.log('Connected to the chat server.');
};

// Handle connection close event
socket.onclose = function(event) {
    console.log('Disconnected from the chat server.', event);
};

// Handle errors
socket.onerror = function(error) {
    console.error('WebSocket error:', error);
};
```

In this code:

- A WebSocket connection is established to the server at ws://localhost:8 080/ws.
- We handle incoming messages by appending them to the message container in the chat window.
- We also log connection events and errors for debugging purposes.

3. Sending Messages

Next, we need to implement the functionality to send messages typed by the user. This will involve capturing the input value from the message input field and sending it to the server through the WebSocket connection.

Example of Sending Messages:

```javascript
// Send message on button click
sendButton.onclick = function() {
    const message = messageInput.value; // Get the message from
    the input field
    if (message) {
        // Send the message as a JSON string
        socket.send(JSON.stringify({ content: message }));
        messageInput.value = ''; // Clear the input field
    }
};

// Alternatively, you can send messages by pressing Enter
messageInput.addEventListener('keypress', function(event) {
    if (event.key === 'Enter') {
        sendButton.click(); // Trigger the click event on the
        send button
    }
});
```

In this example:

- The input value is sent as a JSON string to the server using socket.send().
- After sending the message, the input field is cleared to allow for new messages.
- An event listener is added to allow users to send messages by pressing the Enter key, enhancing the user experience.

4. Enhancing User Experience

To improve the user experience, consider implementing the following features:

- **Message Acknowledgments**: Optionally, you could implement a system that confirms whether a message was successfully sent and displayed on the server.
- **Scrolling to New Messages**: Automatically scroll the chat window to the most recent message to keep the conversation visible.

javascript

```javascript
// Function to scroll to the bottom of the messages container
function scrollToBottom() {
    messagesContainer.scrollTop = messagesContainer.scrollHeight;
}

// Call this function when a new message is received
socket.onmessage = function(event) {
    const message = JSON.parse(event.data);
    const messageElement = document.createElement('div');
    messageElement.textContent = message.content;
    messagesContainer.appendChild(messageElement);
    scrollToBottom(); // Scroll to the bottom after adding a new
    message
};
```

- **Styling the Chat Interface**: Use CSS to improve the appearance of your chat interface. A simple style can enhance readability and user engagement.

Example of Basic CSS Styles (static/styles.css):

css

```css
body {
    font-family: Arial, sans-serif;
    margin: 0;
```

```
    padding: 0;
}

#chat-container {
    width: 400px;
    margin: 0 auto;
    padding: 20px;
    border: 1px solid #ccc;
    border-radius: 5px;
    background-color: #f9f9f9;
}

#messages {
    max-height: 300px;
    overflow-y: auto;
    border: 1px solid #ddd;
    padding: 10px;
    margin-bottom: 10px;
}

#message-input {
    width: 70%;
    padding: 10px;
}

#send-button {
    padding: 10px;
}
```

These styles provide a simple layout for the chat container, messages, and input fields.

5. Testing the Client-Side Logic

With the client-side logic implemented, you can test the application by following these steps:

Run the WebSocket Server: Ensure that your WebSocket server is running by executing the app.py file.

```bash

python app.py
```

Open the Chat Interface: Open your web browser and navigate to the chat application's HTML file (e.g., templates/index.html). If you are serving it using a static server, ensure the server is running.

Test Message Sending: Type messages into the input field and click the send button or press Enter. Verify that messages are displayed in the chat window and are received by all connected clients.

In this section, we have successfully implemented the client-side logic for our asynchronous chat application. By establishing a WebSocket connection, handling user input, sending messages, and enhancing the user experience, we have created a functional chat interface that interacts seamlessly with the WebSocket server.

Testing and Running the Chat Application

Now that we have implemented both the server-side and client-side logic for our asynchronous chat application, it's time to test and run the application. This section will guide you through the process of testing the application for functionality, performance, and user experience, as well as providing troubleshooting tips for common issues.

1. Running the Application

Before testing the application, ensure that both the server and client are set up correctly. Follow these steps to start the application:

Start the WebSocket Server: Open your terminal, navigate to your project directory where the app.py file is located, and run the following command to start the WebSocket server:

```bash

python app.py
```

You should see output indicating that the server is running and listening for connections on localhost at port 8080.

Open the Chat Client: Open your web browser and navigate to the HTML file for the chat application (e.g., templates/index.html). If you are using a static file server, ensure it is running and correctly serving the HTML file.

2. Functional Testing

Once both the server and client are running, you can conduct functional testing to ensure that all features of the chat application work as intended. Here are some key tests to perform:

Establishing Connections:

- Open multiple browser tabs or different browsers and navigate to the chat application. Verify that each tab establishes a WebSocket connection to the server.

Sending and Receiving Messages:

- Type a message in one tab and hit the send button or press Enter. Check if the message appears in all connected tabs.
- Repeat this process with different messages from each tab to ensure that messages are broadcasted correctly.

User Interface Interaction:

- Test the user interface by sending messages quickly and using the Enter key for sending. Ensure that the input field clears after sending a message.

- Resize the browser window to test responsiveness, ensuring that the chat interface remains usable across different screen sizes.

Connection Management:

- Close one of the browser tabs and observe the behavior of the remaining tabs. Verify that the remaining clients continue to function and receive messages from others.

Error Handling:

- Simulate network errors by temporarily disconnecting from the internet or stopping the server. Verify that appropriate error messages are logged in the console and that the client can handle reconnections if implemented.

3. Performance Testing

In addition to functional testing, it's important to evaluate the performance of your chat application, particularly under load:

Simulating Multiple Users:

- Use browser tools or automated testing frameworks to simulate multiple users connecting to the chat application. You can use tools like Apache JMeter or Locust to stress test the WebSocket server by generating concurrent connections and sending messages.

Monitoring Resource Usage:

- While testing, monitor the resource usage of your application (CPU, memory) to identify any bottlenecks or performance issues.

Testing Latency:

- Measure the time it takes for messages to be sent and received across different clients. This will help you understand the responsiveness of your chat application.

4. Troubleshooting Common Issues

While testing, you may encounter some common issues. Here are troubleshooting tips for resolving them:

WebSocket Connection Issues:

- If the client fails to connect to the WebSocket server, check that the server is running and listening on the correct port.
- Verify that the WebSocket URL in your JavaScript matches the server's address and port.

Message Not Received:

- If messages are not being broadcasted, check the logic in your Web-Socket handler on the server. Ensure that all clients are properly added to the clients set and that the broadcasting loop is functioning correctly.

Client Crashes or Unresponsive:

- If the client becomes unresponsive, check for JavaScript errors in the browser's console. Make sure there are no unhandled exceptions, especially in the WebSocket message handlers.

Error Messages:

- Look for error messages in both the server logs and the browser console. These can provide insights into what went wrong, helping you diagnose issues.

Check CORS Issues:

- If you're serving your client files from a different origin than the WebSocket server, ensure that you have appropriate CORS headers set up to allow cross-origin requests.

In this section, we have covered the essential steps for testing and running your asynchronous chat application. By running both the WebSocket server and the client-side interface, performing functional and performance testing, and troubleshooting common issues, you can ensure that your application is robust and ready for users.

As you continue to develop and enhance the chat application, consider implementing additional features such as user authentication, chat history, message timestamps, and notifications. Each of these features can improve user experience and provide valuable functionality for your chat application.

Advanced Asynchronous Patterns

Futures and Tasks in Asyncio
In the realm of asynchronous programming with Python's asyncio, understanding the concepts of futures and tasks is essential for writing efficient and effective code. Futures and tasks provide powerful abstractions for managing asynchronous operations, allowing developers to coordinate and handle multiple concurrent activities seamlessly. This chapter delves into the details of futures and tasks, explaining their roles, how to create and use them, and best practices for leveraging these constructs in your applications.

1. Understanding Futures

A **Future** is an object that represents a value that may not be available yet. It acts as a placeholder for the result of an asynchronous operation. In asyncio, futures are used to manage the results of tasks and to facilitate communication between coroutines. Futures are particularly useful when a result from one coroutine is needed by another, or when a callback needs to be executed once a result is available.

Characteristics of Futures

- **State**: A future can be in one of three states:
- **Pending**: The operation is still in progress, and the result is not yet available.
- **Done**: The operation has completed, either successfully or with an error.

101

- **Cancelled**: The operation was cancelled before it could complete.
- **Callbacks**: You can attach callbacks to a future that will be called when the future is done. This allows for a more event-driven programming style.

Creating a Future

In asyncio, you can create a future using the loop.create_future() method. However, in most cases, you will interact with futures indirectly through tasks, which manage futures automatically.

Example of Creating a Future:

```python
python

import asyncio

async def main():
    loop = asyncio.get_event_loop()
    future = loop.create_future()  # Create a future

    async def set_future_value():
        await asyncio.sleep(1)  # Simulate an asynchronous
        operation
        future.set_result("Future value set!")  # Set the result

    asyncio.create_task(set_future_value())  # Start the task
    result = await future  # Wait for the future to be done
    print(result)  # Output: Future value set!

asyncio.run(main())
```

In this example:

- We create a future and define an asynchronous function that simulates some work before setting the result.
- We use await future to wait for the result, which allows the main coroutine to pause until the value is available.

2. Understanding Tasks

A **Task** is a specialized subclass of a Future that is used to wrap a coroutine. When you create a task, you schedule the execution of the coroutine and immediately receive a Future-like object that represents the result of that coroutine.

Characteristics of Tasks

- **Execution**: Tasks are responsible for executing coroutines in an asynchronous manner. When you create a task, the associated coroutine runs in the event loop.
- **Lifecycle**: Like futures, tasks have a lifecycle consisting of pending, done, and cancelled states. You can check the status of a task and wait for its result.
- **Automatic Handling**: Tasks automatically manage their futures, meaning you don't need to create futures explicitly when working with tasks.

Creating a Task

You can create a task using asyncio.create_task() or loop.create_task(). This schedules the coroutine for execution and returns a Task object.

Example of Creating and Using a Task:

```python
python

import asyncio

async def my_coroutine():
    await asyncio.sleep(1)  # Simulate some work
    return "Task completed!"

async def main():
    task = asyncio.create_task(my_coroutine())  # Create a task
    print("Task has been created.")

    result = await task  # Wait for the task to complete
```

```
    print(result)  # Output: Task completed!

 asyncio.run(main())
```

In this example:

- We define a simple coroutine that simulates work and returns a result.
- We create a task and await its completion, receiving the result when it is done.

3. Handling Task Results and Exceptions

When a task completes, it can either return a result or raise an exception. Proper handling of these outcomes is essential for robust asynchronous programming.

Getting Results

You can retrieve the result of a task by awaiting it. If the task completes successfully, the result is returned. If the task raises an exception, it will propagate when you await the task.

Example of Handling Task Results:

```python
import asyncio

async def successful_task():
    return "Success!"

async def failing_task():
    raise ValueError("An error occurred!")

async def main():
    task1 = asyncio.create_task(successful_task())
    task2 = asyncio.create_task(failing_task())

    try:
```

```
        result1 = await task1
        print(result1)  # Output: Success!

        result2 = await task2  # This will raise an exception
    except Exception as e:
        print(f"Caught an exception: {e}")  # Output: Caught an
        exception: An error occurred!

asyncio.run(main())
```

In this example:

- We create two tasks, one that completes successfully and another that raises an exception.
- We use a try block to catch exceptions from the second task.

Using asyncio.gather()

The asyncio.gather() function can be used to run multiple tasks concurrently and collect their results. If any of the tasks raise an exception, it will propagate, but you can handle it accordingly.

Example of Using asyncio.gather():

```python
python

import asyncio

async def task1():
    await asyncio.sleep(1)
    return "Task 1 completed!"

async def task2():
    await asyncio.sleep(2)
    return "Task 2 completed!"

async def task3():
    await asyncio.sleep(1)
```

```
        raise ValueError("Task 3 encountered an error!")

async def main():
    try:
        results = await asyncio.gather(task1(), task2(), task3())
        print(results)
    except Exception as e:
        print(f"Caught an exception during gather: {e}")

asyncio.run(main())
```

In this example:

- We use asyncio.gather() to run multiple tasks concurrently.
- If task3() raises an exception, it will be caught, and we will print the error message.

4. Best Practices for Using Futures and Tasks

To effectively leverage futures and tasks in your asynchronous applications, consider the following best practices:

1. **Use Tasks for Coroutines**: Whenever you need to run a coroutine, create a task using asyncio.create_task() instead of manually managing futures. This simplifies your code and reduces complexity.
2. **Avoid Blocking the Event Loop**: Ensure that tasks run asynchronously and do not block the event loop. Avoid using synchronous operations within coroutines.
3. **Handle Exceptions Gracefully**: Always handle exceptions from tasks to prevent unexpected crashes. Use try/except blocks and consider using asyncio.gather() with exception handling.
4. **Clean Up Resources**: If your tasks allocate resources (e.g., database connections, files), ensure that you clean up those resources after the task is complete, even if an exception occurs.
5. **Limit Concurrent Tasks**: When dealing with a large number of

concurrent tasks, consider limiting the number of tasks that run simultaneously to avoid overwhelming the system. You can use semaphores for this purpose.

6. **Utilize Callbacks Sparingly**: While you can attach callbacks to futures, consider using async functions and await to maintain readability and avoid callback hell.

Futures and tasks are foundational concepts in asynchronous programming with asyncio, providing a powerful mechanism for managing asynchronous operations in Python. By understanding their characteristics, how to create and manage them, and best practices for handling results and exceptions, you can write efficient, robust asynchronous applications.

Using Coroutines Effectively

Coroutines are a fundamental aspect of asynchronous programming in Python, particularly when using the asyncio library. They allow for non-blocking execution, enabling your applications to perform multiple tasks concurrently without the complexity of traditional threading models. This section will explore best practices for defining, using, and managing coroutines effectively in your applications, ensuring optimal performance and maintainability.

1. Understanding Coroutines

A coroutine is a special type of function defined with the async def syntax. Coroutines can be paused and resumed, allowing the event loop to switch between them, which makes them suitable for asynchronous programming.

Characteristics of Coroutines:

- **Non-blocking**: Coroutines yield control back to the event loop when they reach an await expression, allowing other tasks to run concurrently.
- **Stateful**: Coroutines can maintain state between yields, enabling

complex workflows and interactions.

- **Readable**: Using async and await makes asynchronous code more readable and easier to understand compared to traditional callback-based approaches.

2. Defining Coroutines

When defining coroutines, consider the following best practices to ensure they are effective and maintainable:

Use Descriptive Names

Choose clear and descriptive names for your coroutines to convey their purpose. This practice enhances code readability and helps others (and yourself) understand the code later.

Example:

```python
async def fetch_data_from_api(endpoint):
    # Implementation here
    pass
```

Keep Coroutines Focused

Design coroutines to perform a single, specific task. This principle adheres to the Single Responsibility Principle (SRP) and makes testing and debugging easier.

Example:

```python
async def download_file(url):
    # Logic to download the file from the URL
    pass

async def process_file(file_path):
    # Logic to process the downloaded file
    pass
```

Use await for Asynchronous Operations

Always use the await keyword when calling asynchronous operations within coroutines. This ensures that the coroutine yields control back to the event loop, allowing other tasks to execute.

Example:

```python
async def fetch_and_process_data(url):
    response = await aiohttp.ClientSession().get(url)
    data = await response.json()
    # Process the data here
```

3. Managing Coroutine Lifecycles

Managing the lifecycle of coroutines is crucial for effective asynchronous programming. This includes starting, pausing, resuming, and cancelling coroutines when necessary.

Starting Coroutines

To start a coroutine, you typically use asyncio.create_task() or asyncio.gather(). Both methods schedule the coroutine for execution and return a Task object that represents the ongoing operation.

Example of Starting a Coroutine:

```python
async def main():
    task = asyncio.create_task
(fetch_data_from_api
('https://api.example.
com/data'))
    await task  # Wait for the task to complete
```

Cancelling Coroutines

Sometimes, you may need to cancel a coroutine, especially in scenarios where the user cancels an operation or the application is shutting down.

You can cancel a task using the cancel() method.

Example of Cancelling a Coroutine:

```python
async def long_running_task():
    try:
        while True:
            # Perform work here
            await asyncio.sleep(1)
    except asyncio.CancelledError:
        print("Task was cancelled.")

async def main():
    task = asyncio.create_task(long_running_task())
    await asyncio.sleep(5)  # Let the task run for a while
    task.cancel()  # Cancel the task
    await task  # Await the task to handle cleanup

asyncio.run(main())
```

In this example, we define a long-running task that can be cancelled. The CancelledError exception is caught to perform any necessary cleanup.

4. Handling Errors in Coroutines

Error handling is critical in coroutines to ensure that exceptions are managed gracefully and do not lead to application crashes.

Use Try/Except Blocks

Wrap your coroutine logic in try/except blocks to handle exceptions that may arise during execution.

Example of Error Handling:

```python
async def safe_fetch(url):
    try:
```

```
async with aiohttp.ClientSession() as session:
    async with session.get(url) as response:
        response.raise_for_status()
# Raise an error for bad responses
        return await response.json()
except aiohttp.ClientError as e:
    print(f"Error fetching data: {e}")
```

In this example, we catch aiohttp.ClientError exceptions to handle any issues that occur during the fetching process.

Logging Errors

Consider logging errors instead of simply printing them to the console. This practice allows you to keep a record of issues that occur in production, making it easier to diagnose and fix problems.

Example of Logging Errors:

```python

import logging

logging.basicConfig(level=logging.ERROR)

async def safe_fetch(url):
    try:
        async with aiohttp.ClientSession() as session:
            async with session.get(url) as response:
                response.raise_for_status()
                return await response.json()
    except aiohttp.ClientError as e:
        logging.error(f"Error fetching data: {e}")
```

In this example, we configure logging to capture error messages, providing a better mechanism for monitoring issues.

5. Using Async Context Managers

Async context managers can be used to manage resources more effectively within coroutines, ensuring that resources are properly cleaned up when no longer needed. Use async with statements to manage the lifecycle of resources.

Example of Using Async Context Managers:

```python
python

async def fetch_data(url):
    async with aiohttp.ClientSession() as session:
        async with session.get(url) as response:
            response.raise_for_status()
            return await response.json()

async def main():
    data = await fetch_data
('https://api.example.com/data')
    print(data)

asyncio.run(main())
```

In this example, aiohttp.ClientSession() and the session.get(url) are both managed using async context managers, ensuring proper resource management.

Using coroutines effectively is essential for building responsive and efficient asynchronous applications in Python. By adhering to best practices for defining coroutines, managing their lifecycles, handling errors gracefully, and utilizing async context managers, you can create robust applications that make the most of Python's asynchronous capabilities.

The Gather and Wait Functions

In asynchronous programming with Python's asyncio, gather and wait are two powerful functions that facilitate the concurrent execution of coroutines and help manage the results of multiple asynchronous tasks. Understanding how to use these functions effectively is essential for optimizing your asynchronous applications. This section will delve into both functions, providing detailed explanations, usage examples, and best practices.

1. Using asyncio.gather()

The asyncio.gather() function allows you to run multiple coroutines concurrently and aggregate their results into a single future. It is especially useful when you want to execute several tasks simultaneously and wait for all of them to complete before proceeding.

Characteristics of asyncio.gather()

- **Concurrency**: gather() runs the specified coroutines concurrently, which can lead to performance improvements compared to running them sequentially.
- **Return Values**: The results of the gathered coroutines are returned in the order they were provided to gather(), even if they complete in a different order.
- **Error Handling**: If any of the gathered coroutines raise an exception, gather() will raise the first exception encountered. You can catch and handle this exception as needed.

Example of Using asyncio.gather()

Here's a basic example demonstrating how to use asyncio.gather() to run multiple asynchronous tasks:

```python
import asyncio

async def fetch_data(id):
    await asyncio.sleep(1)  # Simulate an asynchronous operation
    return f"Data from task {id}"

async def main():
    tasks = [fetch_data(i) for i in range(5)]
```

```
# Create a list of tasks
    results = await asyncio.gather(*tasks)
 # Gather results from all tasks
    print(results)  # Output:
['Data from task 0', 'Data from task 1', ...]

asyncio.run(main())
```

In this example:

- We define a simple coroutine fetch_data() that simulates fetching data.
- We create a list of tasks and use asyncio.gather(*tasks) to run them concurrently.
- The results from all tasks are printed after all have completed.

Error Handling with asyncio.gather()

You can handle errors raised by the gathered coroutines using a try-except block around the gather() call. If any coroutine raises an exception, it will propagate when you await the gather() call.

Example of Error Handling:

```python
async def failing_task():
    await asyncio.sleep(1)
    raise ValueError("An error occurred in the task!")

async def main():
    tasks = [fetch_data(i) for i in range(5)] + [failing_task()]
    # Include a failing task
    try:
        results = await asyncio.gather(*tasks)  # This will raise
        an exception
    except Exception as e:
        print(f"An exception occurred: {e}")
```

```
asyncio.run(main())
```

In this example:

- A failing_task() coroutine is added to the list of tasks.
- If this task raises an exception, it is caught in the except block, allowing you to handle the error gracefully.

2. Using asyncio.wait()

The asyncio.wait() function provides a more flexible way to manage multiple coroutines, giving you control over the execution and completion of tasks. Unlike gather(), which waits for all tasks to finish and returns their results, wait() allows you to choose whether to wait for all tasks to complete or return as soon as any task is finished.

Characteristics of asyncio.wait()

- **Return Types**: wait() returns two sets of tasks: one for the completed tasks and another for the pending tasks. This allows you to take different actions based on the completion state of each task.
- **Completion Behavior**: You can specify how wait() should behave using the return_when parameter, which can be set to asyncio.ALL_COMPLE TED, asyncio.FIRST_COMPLETED, or asyncio.FIRST_EXCEPTION.
- **Task Cancellation**: Tasks that have not completed can be cancelled after waiting.

Example of Using asyncio.wait()

Here's an example that demonstrates how to use asyncio.wait():

python

```
async def task_with_delay(id, delay):
    await asyncio.sleep(delay)  # Simulate a task with a specific
    delay
```

```python
    return f"Task {id} completed!"

async def main():
    tasks = [task_with_delay(i, i) for i in range(5)]  # Tasks
    with increasing delays
    done, pending = await asyncio.wait(tasks,
    return_when=asyncio.FIRST_COMPLETED)

    for task in done:
        print(task.result())  # Print results of completed tasks

    print(f"Pending tasks: {len(pending)}")

asyncio.run(main())
```

In this example:

- We define a coroutine task_with_delay() that simulates a task with a specified delay.
- We use asyncio.wait() to run the tasks and wait for the first one to complete.
- The results of completed tasks are printed, and the number of pending tasks is displayed.

Handling Task Completion

You can also handle completed and pending tasks separately after calling wait(). This allows you to take different actions based on the completion state.

Example of Handling Completion and Cancellation:

```
python
```

```python
async def cancellable_task():
    try:
        await asyncio.sleep(5)
```

```
        return "This task completed."
    except asyncio.CancelledError:
        return "Task was cancelled."

async def main():
    task = asyncio.create_task(cancellable_task())
    await asyncio.sleep(1)  # Let the task run for a bit
    task.cancel()  # Cancel the task
    done, pending = await asyncio.wait([task])  # Wait for
    cancellation to complete

    for t in done:
        print(t.result())  # Check the result of the completed
        task

asyncio.run(main())
```

In this example:

- A task is created that simulates a long-running operation.
- The task is cancelled after a short delay, and we wait for it to complete using wait().
- We check the result of the task to see if it was cancelled.

3. Best Practices for Using gather and wait

To effectively utilize asyncio.gather() and asyncio.wait() in your applications, consider the following best practices:

1. **Use gather() for Simplicity**: When you need to run multiple tasks and aggregate their results, prefer asyncio.gather(). It is straightforward and handles success and failure cases elegantly.
2. **Utilize wait() for Flexibility**: Use asyncio.wait() when you need more control over task execution, such as managing cancellation or handling tasks as they complete.
3. **Monitor and Log Task States**: Implement logging to monitor the status of tasks, especially in production applications. This helps in

diagnosing issues related to performance or errors.

4. **Limit Concurrent Tasks**: If you anticipate running a large number of concurrent tasks, consider limiting the number of active tasks using semaphores to prevent overwhelming the system.

5. **Handle Exceptions Gracefully**: Always implement error handling for tasks that may fail. Use try-except blocks around gather() and manage exceptions from wait() properly.

The asyncio.gather() and asyncio.wait() functions are powerful tools for managing concurrent coroutines in Python's asynchronous programming model. By understanding their characteristics, how to use them effectively, and best practices for error handling and performance optimization, you can write efficient and robust asynchronous applications.

Creating Custom Asynchronous Generators

Asynchronous generators are a powerful feature in Python that combines the benefits of asynchronous programming with the ability to yield values over time, similar to regular generators. This allows for efficient, non-blocking iteration over data that may not be available all at once, such as data from an API, sensor readings, or any other asynchronous data stream. In this section, we will explore how to create custom asynchronous generators, their use cases, and best practices for implementing them.

1. Understanding Asynchronous Generators

An asynchronous generator is defined using the async def syntax and utilizes the yield statement to yield values. Unlike standard generators, which block execution while waiting for the next value, asynchronous generators can yield values while allowing other coroutines to run, providing a more responsive program flow.

Characteristics of Asynchronous Generators

- **Asynchronous Iteration**: Asynchronous generators support the async for syntax, enabling iteration over the yielded values in an asynchronous context.
- **Non-blocking**: While waiting for the next value to be produced, an asynchronous generator can yield control back to the event loop, allowing other tasks to execute.
- **Stateful**: Similar to regular generators, asynchronous generators maintain their state across invocations.

Creating an Asynchronous Generator

To create an asynchronous generator, define a function using the async def syntax and use yield to return values. The await keyword can be used within the generator to perform asynchronous operations before yielding a value.

Example of a Simple Asynchronous Generator

Here's a basic example demonstrating how to create and use an asynchronous generator:

```python
import asyncio

async def async_counter(limit):
    """An asynchronous generator that counts up to a limit."""
    for i in range(limit):
        await asyncio.sleep(1)  # Simulate an asynchronous
        operation
        yield i  # Yield the current count

async def main():
    async for number in async_counter(5):
        print(f"Counted: {number}")

asyncio.run(main())
```

In this example:

- The async_counter function is defined as an asynchronous generator that counts up to a specified limit.
- Inside the generator, await asyncio.sleep(1) simulates an asynchronous delay before yielding the current count.
- In the main() coroutine, we use async for to iterate over the values produced by the generator.

3. Use Cases for Asynchronous Generators

Asynchronous generators are useful in various scenarios, especially when dealing with streaming data or producing values over time. Some common use cases include:

Streaming Data: For applications that consume data streams (e.g., real-time logging, sensor data), asynchronous generators can yield data as it becomes available.

Polling APIs: When periodically polling an API for updates, asynchronous generators can yield responses over time without blocking the event loop.

Batch Processing: For processing large datasets in batches, an asynchronous generator can yield batches of data asynchronously, allowing for efficient processing while maintaining responsiveness.

Implementing Custom Asynchronous Generators

When creating custom asynchronous generators, consider the following best practices:

Handling Cleanup

Use try/finally blocks within your asynchronous generators to perform cleanup actions when the generator is exhausted or closed. This ensures that resources are released properly.

Example of Cleanup in an Asynchronous Generator:

```
python
```

```python
async def async_data_stream():
    """An asynchronous generator that yields data."""
    try:
        for i in range(5):
            await asyncio.sleep(1)  # Simulate data generation
            yield i
    finally:
        print("Cleaning up resources...")

async def main():
    async for data in async_data_stream():
        print(f"Received: {data}")

asyncio.run(main())
```

In this example:

- The finally block executes cleanup actions after the generator has been exhausted.

Using asyncio.Queue with Asynchronous Generators

Asynchronous generators can be integrated with asyncio.Queue to produce and consume items concurrently. This is particularly useful for producer-consumer patterns.

Example of Using asyncio.Queue with an Asynchronous Generator:

python

```python
import asyncio

async def producer(queue):
    """An asynchronous generator that produces items."""
    for i in range(5):
        await asyncio.sleep(1)  # Simulate production delay
        await queue.put(i)  # Put item in the queue
        print(f"Produced: {i}")
```

```python
async def consumer(queue):
    """An asynchronous consumer that consumes items."""
    while True:
        item = await queue.get()  # Get item from the queue
        if item is None:  # Exit signal
            break
        print(f"Consumed: {item}")
        queue.task_done()  # Mark the task as done

async def main():
    queue = asyncio.Queue()
    await asyncio.gather(producer(queue), consumer(queue))

asyncio.run(main())
```

In this example:

- The producer() coroutine produces items and places them into an asyncio.Queue.
- The consumer() coroutine retrieves and processes items from the queue asynchronously.
- The queue allows for decoupling production and consumption, enhancing the responsiveness of the application.

Custom asynchronous generators provide a powerful mechanism for managing asynchronous data streams in Python. By defining generators using the async def syntax and leveraging the yield statement, you can create responsive applications that handle data efficiently without blocking the event loop.

Debugging Asynchronous Code

Debugging asynchronous code can be more challenging than debugging synchronous code due to the complexity introduced by concurrency and the non-linear execution flow. However, with the right techniques and tools, you can effectively troubleshoot issues in your asynchronous applications. This section will explore strategies for debugging asynchronous code, including using logging, handling exceptions, and leveraging built-in debugging tools.

1. Common Challenges in Debugging Asynchronous Code

Before diving into debugging techniques, it's essential to understand some of the common challenges you may encounter when working with asynchronous code:

- **Non-linear Execution Flow**: The asynchronous nature of coroutines means that the order of execution can be unpredictable. This makes it harder to trace the flow of logic and identify where things go wrong.
- **Race Conditions**: Concurrent tasks may interact in unexpected ways, leading to race conditions where the outcome depends on the timing of operations.
- **State Management**: Maintaining and tracking state across multiple asynchronous operations can be complex, particularly if tasks depend on each other.
- **Error Handling**: Exceptions raised in asynchronous code can be harder to catch and trace back, especially if they occur in callbacks or in tasks that run in the background.

2. Using Logging for Debugging

One of the most effective ways to debug asynchronous code is by using logging. The Python logging module provides a flexible framework for emitting log messages from your applications.

Configuring Logging

Start by configuring the logging system at the beginning of your script. You can set the logging level, format, and output destination.

Example of Configuring Logging:

```python
python

import logging

# Configure logging
logging.basicConfig(level=logging.DEBUG, format='%(asctime)s -
%(levelname)s - %(message)s')
```

In this example, we set the logging level to DEBUG, which allows all messages at this level and higher to be logged. We also specify a format that includes the timestamp, log level, and message.

Adding Logging Statements

Incorporate logging statements throughout your asynchronous code to trace execution and capture important information.

Example of Adding Logging to an Asynchronous Function:

```python
python

import asyncio
import logging

async def fetch_data(url):
    logging.debug(f"Starting fetch for {url}")
    await asyncio.sleep(1)  # Simulate network delay
    logging.debug(f"Finished fetch for {url}")
    return f"Data from {url}"

async def main():
    urls = ['http://example.com/data1',
    'http://example.com/data2']
    for url in urls:
        data = await fetch_data(url)
        logging.info(f"Received: {data}")

asyncio.run(main())
```

In this example:

- Logging statements are added to indicate when a fetch starts and finishes, providing visibility into the flow of execution.
- We log the received data at the INFO level, which is helpful for understanding the output of the program.

3. Handling Exceptions

Properly handling exceptions in asynchronous code is crucial for debugging. Ensure that you catch exceptions in coroutines and log them appropriately.

Using Try/Except Blocks

Wrap your asynchronous operations in try/except blocks to catch exceptions and log error messages.

Example of Exception Handling:

python

```python
async def safe_fetch(url):
    try:
        data = await fetch_data(url)
        return data
    except Exception as e:
        logging.error(f"Error fetching data from {url}: {e}")

async def main():
    urls = ['http://example.com/data1',
    'http://example.com/data2', 'http://invalid-url']
    tasks = [safe_fetch(url) for url in urls]
    await asyncio.gather(*tasks)

asyncio.run(main())
```

In this example:

- The safe_fetch function logs any exceptions that occur during the fetching process, allowing you to track down errors effectively.

Logging Task Exceptions

When using asyncio.gather(), you can catch exceptions raised by individual tasks by wrapping the entire gather() call in a try/except block.

Example of Logging Task Exceptions:

```python

async def main():
    tasks = [fetch_data(url) for url in urls]
    try:
        await asyncio.gather(*tasks)
    except Exception as e:
        logging.error(f"One of the tasks raised an exception:
        {e}")

asyncio.run(main())
```

This approach allows you to log errors from any of the tasks executed in the gather() call.

4. Using Built-in Debugging Tools

Python's asyncio module provides built-in debugging capabilities that can help identify issues in your asynchronous code. By enabling debugging mode, you can get detailed information about task states and the event loop.

Enabling Debug Mode

You can enable debug mode by setting the debug parameter when creating the event loop:

```python

asyncio.run(main(), debug=True)
```

Alternatively, you can enable debugging globally:

```python
import asyncio

asyncio.get_event_loop().set_debug(True)
```

In debug mode, asyncio will emit warnings and additional logging related to the execution of tasks and the event loop, which can help diagnose problems.

Using asyncio.Task.all_tasks()

The asyncio.Task.all_tasks() method returns a set of all tasks that are currently active. This can be useful for inspecting the state of tasks and identifying those that are still pending or have completed.

Example of Inspecting Active Tasks:

```python
async def main():
    tasks = [fetch_data(url) for url in urls]
    await asyncio.gather(*tasks)
    active_tasks = asyncio.all_tasks()
    logging.info(f"Active tasks: {active_tasks}")

asyncio.run(main())
```

In this example, we log the active tasks after executing the gathered tasks.

5. Best Practices for Debugging Asynchronous Code

To effectively debug your asynchronous applications, consider the following best practices:

1. **Use Logging**: Incorporate logging throughout your code to capture execution flow, errors, and important state information. This will help you diagnose issues effectively.
2. **Handle Exceptions**: Always catch and log exceptions in your coroutines to understand what went wrong. Use try/except blocks around

critical sections of your code.

3. **Enable Debug Mode**: Use asyncio's built-in debugging features to get insights into task states and the event loop behavior.

4. **Test Incrementally**: Test your asynchronous code incrementally to catch issues early. Start with smaller pieces of functionality before integrating larger parts of your application.

5. **Leverage Debuggers**: Use interactive debuggers like pdb or IDE features that support asynchronous code debugging. This allows you to step through your code and inspect variables in real time.

6. **Monitor Performance**: Keep an eye on performance metrics, especially if your application processes a large number of tasks concurrently. Profiling tools can help identify bottlenecks.

Debugging asynchronous code requires a different approach compared to traditional synchronous programming due to the complexities of concurrency and the non-linear execution flow. By using logging effectively, handling exceptions gracefully, enabling built-in debugging tools, and following best practices, you can troubleshoot issues in your asynchronous applications more effectively.

Real-Time Data Processing with Websockets

U nderstanding Websockets
    Websockets are a protocol that provides full-duplex communication channels over a single TCP connection. This technology enables real-time interaction between clients (typically web browsers) and servers, allowing for more dynamic and responsive applications compared to traditional HTTP communication. This chapter will explore the WebSocket protocol in detail, including its characteristics, advantages, and typical use cases, setting the stage for implementing real-time data processing in your applications.

1. What are Websockets?

Websockets allow for interactive communication sessions between a user's browser and a server. Unlike traditional HTTP requests, where communication is limited to request-response pairs, Websockets enable a persistent connection that can be used for sending and receiving messages in real time.

How Websockets Work

The WebSocket protocol begins with a handshake initiated by the client. After the handshake, the connection is established and kept open, allowing both parties to send messages at any time without the need to re-establish the connection.

- **Handshake Process**: The handshake involves an initial HTTP request from the client to the server, requesting an upgrade to the WebSocket protocol. If the server accepts the request, it responds with an HTTP 101 status code, indicating that the protocol has been switched.
- **Data Frames**: Once the connection is established, data is transmitted in frames, which are small packets of data. WebSockets use a specific framing structure that includes information about the type of data being sent (e.g., text, binary).
- **Full-Duplex Communication**: The connection supports full-duplex communication, meaning that messages can be sent and received simultaneously. This capability is particularly useful for applications that require real-time updates.

2. Key Characteristics of Websockets

Websockets offer several key features that make them suitable for real-time applications:

Low Latency

Websockets maintain a persistent connection, which reduces the latency associated with establishing new connections for each request. This results in faster message delivery and a more responsive user experience.

Reduced Overhead

After the initial handshake, Websockets eliminate the need for HTTP headers with each message. This reduction in overhead allows for smaller message sizes and more efficient communication.

Event-Driven Communication

Websockets support an event-driven model, where the server can push messages to the client as soon as they become available. This capability is essential for applications like chat systems, live notifications, and real-time dashboards.

Cross-Origin Communication

Websockets support cross-origin communication, allowing web applications hosted on different domains to communicate seamlessly, provided the server allows it through appropriate CORS (Cross-Origin Resource

Sharing) configurations.

3. Advantages of Websockets

The use of Websockets offers several advantages over traditional HTTP communication, especially for applications that require real-time interactions:

Real-Time Data Exchange

Websockets enable instantaneous data exchange, making them ideal for applications that need to deliver live updates, such as stock tickers, online gaming, and social media feeds.

Efficient Resource Utilization

By maintaining a persistent connection, Websockets reduce the resource overhead associated with creating and tearing down multiple HTTP connections. This efficiency is particularly beneficial in applications with high-frequency message exchanges.

Enhanced User Experience

The responsiveness afforded by Websockets leads to a more engaging user experience. Users receive updates without needing to refresh or poll the server, resulting in smoother interactions.

Scalability

Websockets are scalable and can handle numerous concurrent connections efficiently. This capability is crucial for applications that expect high user engagement, such as chat applications or collaborative tools.

4. Typical Use Cases for Websockets

Websockets are well-suited for a variety of real-time applications. Some common use cases include:

Chat Applications

Websockets are extensively used in chat applications to enable real-time messaging between users. The persistent connection allows messages to be sent and received instantly, creating a seamless communication experience.

Live Notifications and Alerts

Applications that provide real-time notifications, such as social media platforms or news websites, can utilize Websockets to push updates to users as soon as they occur.

Online Gaming

Websockets are ideal for online multiplayer games, where players need to receive updates on game state and player actions in real time. The low latency and efficient data exchange are critical for maintaining a smooth gaming experience.

Financial Applications

Websockets are commonly used in financial applications, such as stock trading platforms, where real-time price updates and market data are essential for decision-making.

Collaborative Tools

In collaborative applications like document editors or project management tools, Websockets facilitate real-time collaboration, allowing multiple users to see changes instantly as they are made.

Websockets represent a powerful technology for enabling real-time communication in web applications. By providing low-latency, efficient, and event-driven data exchange, Websockets are well-suited for a variety of use cases that require instantaneous updates and interactivity.

Setting Up a WebSocket Server with Aiohttp

Now that we understand the fundamentals of WebSockets, we will focus on how to implement a WebSocket server using the aiohttp library in Python. This section will guide you through the process of setting up the server, handling client connections, managing messages, and ensuring robust communication between clients.

1. Installing Aiohttp

Before we begin, ensure that you have the aiohttp library installed in your Python environment. If you haven't done so yet, you can install it using pip:

```bash
pip install aiohttp
```

2. Creating the WebSocket Server

To create a WebSocket server using aiohttp, you will define an asynchronous WebSocket handler that manages client connections and message exchanges. Below are the steps to set up the server.

Importing Required Libraries

Start by creating a new Python file (e.g., websocket_server.py) and import the necessary modules.

```python
import asyncio
from aiohttp import web
```

Defining the WebSocket Handler

Create a WebSocket handler function that will manage the connections from clients. This function will handle incoming messages, broadcast messages to all connected clients, and clean up connections when clients disconnect.

Example of a WebSocket Handler:

```python
clients = set()  # A set to keep track of connected clients

async def websocket_handler(request):
    ws = web.WebSocketResponse()  # Create a WebSocket response
    await ws.prepare(request)  # Prepare the WebSocket connection
    clients.add(ws)  # Add the new client to the set of connected
    clients

    try:
```

```
    async for msg in ws:  # Listen for incoming messages
        if msg.type == web.WSMsgType.TEXT:
            # Broadcast the received message to all connected
            clients
            for client in clients:
                if client is not ws:  # Don't send the
                message back to the sender
                    await client.send_str(msg.data)  # Send
                    the message to the client
        elif msg.type == web.WSMsgType.ERROR:
            print(f'WebSocket error: {ws.exception()}')
    finally:
        clients.remove(ws)  # Remove the client when disconnected
        await ws.close()  # Close the WebSocket connection

    return ws
```

In this handler:

- We create a WebSocketResponse object and prepare it for incoming connections.
- The new client is added to the clients set.
- We listen for incoming messages using an asynchronous loop (async for).
- When a message is received, it is broadcast to all other connected clients, and we handle potential errors.

Setting Up the Application

After defining the WebSocket handler, you need to set up the web application and define the route for the WebSocket connection.

Example of Setting Up the Application:

python

```
async def init_app():
    app = web.Application()  # Create a new web application
```

```python
app.router.add_get('/ws', websocket_handler)  # Define the
route for WebSocket connections
return app
```

In this function, we create an instance of web.Application() and add a route that points to the WebSocket handler.

Running the WebSocket Server

Finally, you need to run the server and start listening for incoming WebSocket connections. Add the following code to your websocket_server.py file:

python

```python
if __name__ == '__main__':
    app = asyncio.run(init_app())  # Initialize the application
    web.run_app(app, host='localhost', port=8080)  # Run the app
    on the specified host and port
```

This code initializes the application and starts the web server, which listens for incoming WebSocket connections on localhost at port 8080.

3. Complete WebSocket Server Code

Here's the complete code for the WebSocket server:

python

```python
import asyncio
from aiohttp import web

clients = set()  # Set to keep track of connected clients

async def websocket_handler(request):
    ws = web.WebSocketResponse()  # Create a WebSocket response
    await ws.prepare(request)  # Prepare the WebSocket connection
    clients.add(ws)  # Add the new client to the set of connected
```

```
    clients

    try:
        async for msg in ws:  # Listen for incoming messages
            if msg.type == web.WSMsgType.TEXT:
                # Broadcast the received message to all connected
                clients
                for client in clients:
                    if client is not ws:  # Don't send the
                    message back to the sender
                        await client.send_str(msg.data)  # Send
                        the message to the client
            elif msg.type == web.WSMsgType.ERROR:
                print(f'WebSocket error: {ws.exception()}')
    finally:
        clients.remove(ws)  # Remove the client when disconnected
        await ws.close()  # Close the WebSocket connection

    return ws

async def init_app():
    app = web.Application()  # Create a new web application
    app.router.add_get('/ws', websocket_handler)  # Define the
    route for WebSocket connections
    return app

if __name__ == '__main__':
    app = asyncio.run(init_app())  # Initialize the application
    web.run_app(app, host='localhost', port=8080)  # Run the app
    on the specified host and port
```

4. Testing the WebSocket Server

To test the WebSocket server, you can create a simple HTML client that connects to the WebSocket server and sends/receives messages. Here's an example of a simple client you can use:

HTML Client Example (index.html):

html

```html
<!DOCTYPE html>
<html lang="en">
<head>
    <meta charset="UTF-8">
    <meta name="viewport" content="width=device-width,
    initial-scale=1.0">
    <title>WebSocket Chat Client</title>
</head>
<body>
    <h1>WebSocket Chat Client</h1>
    <input type="text" id="messageInput" placeholder="Type a
    message..." autocomplete="off">
    <button id="sendButton">Send</button>
    <div id="messages"></div>

    <script>
        const ws = new WebSocket('ws://localhost:8080/ws');  //
        Connect to WebSocket server
        const messageInput =
        document.getElementById('messageInput');
        const sendButton = document.getElementById('sendButton');
        const messagesDiv = document.getElementById('messages');

        ws.onmessage = function(event) {
            const message = document.createElement('div');
            message.textContent = event.data;  // Display the
            received message
            messagesDiv.appendChild(message);
        };

        sendButton.onclick = function() {
            const message = messageInput.value;
            if (message) {
                ws.send(message);  // Send the message to the
                server
                messageInput.value = '';  // Clear the input field
            }
        };
```

```
    </script>
  </body>
  </html>
```

To test the WebSocket server:

Start the server by running the websocket_server.py script:

```bash

python websocket_server.py
```

Open the index.html file in a web browser (you can use a local web server to serve it if necessary).

Type messages in the input field and click the send button. Open multiple browser tabs or windows to test message broadcasting between clients.

In this section, we have successfully set up a WebSocket server using the aiohttp library. By implementing a WebSocket handler, managing client connections, and broadcasting messages, we have created the foundation for real-time communication between users.

Building a Real-Time Data Dashboard

In this section, we will walk through the process of building a real-time data dashboard using WebSockets and aiohttp. The dashboard will dynamically display data updates, allowing users to visualize information as it changes in real time. We will cover the setup of the server, the client-side implementation, and how to integrate real-time data feeds into the dashboard.

1. Overview of the Real-Time Data Dashboard

The goal of our real-time data dashboard is to create an interactive web interface that:

- Displays incoming data in real time using WebSockets.
- Provides visual elements, such as charts and tables, to represent the data.
- Updates automatically as new data arrives without requiring manual refreshes.

For this example, we will simulate incoming data updates (e.g., stock prices or sensor readings) using our WebSocket server.

2. Setting Up the Server

We will extend our existing WebSocket server to generate and send random data updates to connected clients. This will simulate real-time data streams that the dashboard will display.

Extending the WebSocket Handler

Modify the WebSocket handler in your websocket_server.py to periodically send random data updates to connected clients.

Example of Extended WebSocket Handler:

```python
import asyncio
import random
from aiohttp import web

clients = set()  # Set to keep track of connected clients

async def generate_data():
    """Simulate generating random data."""
    while True:
        await asyncio.sleep(2)  # Wait for 2 seconds between
        updates
        data = {
            'sensor_id': 1,
```

```python
                'value': random.uniform(20.0, 100.0)  # Simulate a
                random sensor value
            }
            # Broadcast the data to all connected clients
            for client in clients:
                await client.send_json(data)

async def websocket_handler(request):
    ws = web.WebSocketResponse()
    await ws.prepare(request)
    clients.add(ws)

    # Start the data generator coroutine
    asyncio.create_task(generate_data())

    try:
        async for msg in ws:
            if msg.type == web.WSMsgType.ERROR:
                print(f'WebSocket error: {ws.exception()}')
    finally:
        clients.remove(ws)
        await ws.close()

    return ws

async def init_app():
    app = web.Application()
    app.router.add_get('/ws', websocket_handler)
    return app

if __name__ == '__main__':
    app = asyncio.run(init_app())
    web.run_app(app, host='localhost', port=8080)
```

In this code:

- We define a generate_data() coroutine that simulates the generation of random data every 2 seconds.
- Each generated data point is sent to all connected clients using

send_json(), which sends the data as a JSON object.

3. Building the Client-Side Dashboard

Now, we'll create the client-side dashboard that connects to the Web-Socket server and visualizes the data in real time.

Creating the HTML Dashboard

Create an HTML file (e.g., dashboard.html) for the client interface. This dashboard will connect to the WebSocket server and display the incoming data updates.

Example of HTML Dashboard:

```html
html

<!DOCTYPE html>
<html lang="en">
<head>
    <meta charset="UTF-8">
    <meta name="viewport" content="width=device-width,
    initial-scale=1.0">
    <title>Real-Time Data Dashboard</title>
    <style>
        body {
            font-family: Arial, sans-serif;
        }
        #data-container {
            margin: 20px;
        }
        .data-item {
            padding: 10px;
            border: 1px solid #ccc;
            margin-bottom: 10px;
            border-radius: 5px;
        }
    </style>
</head>
<body>
    <h1>Real-Time Data Dashboard</h1>
```

```html
    <div id="data-container"></div>

    <script>
        const ws = new WebSocket('ws://localhost:8080/ws');  //
        Connect to WebSocket server
        const dataContainer =
        document.getElementById('data-container');

        ws.onmessage = function(event) {
            const data = JSON.parse(event.data);  // Parse the
            incoming JSON data
            const dataItem = document.createElement('div');
            dataItem.className = 'data-item';
            dataItem.textContent = `Sensor ID: ${data.sensor_id},
            Value: ${data.value.toFixed(2)}`;  // Display the data
            dataContainer.appendChild(dataItem);  // Append the
            data item to the container
        };

        ws.onopen = function() {
            console.log('Connected to the WebSocket server.');
        };

        ws.onclose = function() {
            console.log('Disconnected from the WebSocket
            server.');
        };

        ws.onerror = function(error) {
            console.error('WebSocket error:', error);
        };
    </script>
  </body>
  </html>
```

In this HTML file:

- We create a simple layout with a header and a container to display incoming data.

- The JavaScript section connects to the WebSocket server and listens for incoming messages.
- When data is received, it is parsed and displayed in the data-container.

4. Testing the Real-Time Data Dashboard

To test your real-time data dashboard, follow these steps:

Start the WebSocket Server: Run your websocket_server.py script to start the server.

```bash
python websocket_server.py
```

Open the Dashboard: Open the dashboard.html file in your web browser. If you're using a local server, ensure it's serving this HTML file correctly.

Observe Real-Time Data: The dashboard should connect to the Web-Socket server and begin displaying simulated data updates every two seconds.

5. Enhancing the Dashboard

Once you have the basic dashboard up and running, you can consider adding more features to improve functionality and user experience:

Data Visualization: Integrate libraries like Chart.js or D3.js to create visual representations (charts, graphs) of the incoming data.

Historical Data: Store incoming data in a database (e.g., SQLite, PostgreSQL) and provide options to view historical trends.

Filtering and Sorting: Allow users to filter or sort the displayed data based on specific criteria (e.g., by sensor ID or value range).

User Authentication: Implement user authentication to restrict access to the dashboard, ensuring that only authorized users can view sensitive data.

Responsive Design: Use CSS frameworks like Bootstrap to make the dashboard responsive, enhancing usability across devices.

In this section, we successfully built a real-time data dashboard using WebSockets and aiohttp. By setting up a WebSocket server to send simulated data updates and creating a client-side dashboard to display this data, we demonstrated how to implement real-time data processing in a web application.

Handling Multiple Connections

In a real-time application utilizing WebSockets, handling multiple concurrent connections is crucial for ensuring that all clients can interact with the server simultaneously and receive real-time updates. In this section, we will explore strategies for managing multiple connections efficiently using the aiohttp library, covering topics such as client management, broadcasting messages, and optimizing performance for high concurrency scenarios.

1. Client Management

To handle multiple connections, it is essential to maintain a record of all connected clients. This allows the server to broadcast messages and manage interactions effectively.

Storing Connected Clients

As shown in previous examples, you can use a set to keep track of connected WebSocket clients. Each time a client connects, you add it to the set, and when it disconnects, you remove it.

Example of Managing Clients:

```python
python

clients = set()  # Set to keep track of connected clients

async def websocket_handler(request):
    ws = web.WebSocketResponse()
    await ws.prepare(request)
    clients.add(ws)  # Add the new client
```

```
try:
    async for msg in ws:
        # Handle incoming messages here
        pass
finally:
    clients.remove(ws)  # Remove the client when disconnected
    await ws.close()
```

2. Broadcasting Messages

When a client sends a message, you may want to broadcast that message to all other connected clients. This involves iterating over the set of connected clients and sending the message to each one.

Example of Broadcasting Messages

Here's an example of how to broadcast messages received from one client to all other connected clients:

python

```
async def websocket_handler(request):
    ws = web.WebSocketResponse()
    await ws.prepare(request)
    clients.add(ws)

    try:
        async for msg in ws:
            if msg.type == web.WSMsgType.TEXT:
                # Broadcast the message to all other clients
                for client in clients:
                    if client is not ws:  # Don't send the
                    message back to the sender
                        await client.send_str(msg.data)
    finally:
        clients.remove(ws)
        await ws.close()
```

In this example:

- When a message is received, we loop through the clients set and send the message to each client except the one that sent it.

3. Managing High Concurrency

When handling many connections, it's important to consider performance and resource management. Here are some strategies to optimize your WebSocket server for high concurrency:

Using Efficient Data Structures

Sets are efficient for storing connected clients due to their average O(1) time complexity for adding and removing elements. This ensures that operations on client connections remain performant, even with many clients.

Limiting Concurrent Connections

You may need to limit the number of concurrent connections to avoid overwhelming your server. You can implement a simple semaphore mechanism to limit the number of simultaneous connections.

Example of Limiting Connections:

python

```
sem = asyncio.Semaphore(100)  # Limit to 100 concurrent
connections

async def websocket_handler(request):
    async with sem:  # Ensure that we acquire the semaphore
        ws = web.WebSocketResponse()
        await ws.prepare(request)
        clients.add(ws)

        try:
            async for msg in ws:
                # Handle messages here
                pass
        finally:
            clients.remove(ws)
            await ws.close()
```

In this example:

- We create a semaphore that limits concurrent connections to 100. The async with sem: statement ensures that only the allowed number of clients can connect simultaneously.

Handling Timeouts and Connection Drops

WebSocket connections may drop unexpectedly, either due to network issues or client behavior. Implementing timeouts and graceful handling of dropped connections is essential.

Example of Handling Connection Drops:

python

```python
async def websocket_handler(request):
    ws = web.WebSocketResponse()
    await ws.prepare(request)
    clients.add(ws)

    try:
        async for msg in ws:
            if msg.type == web.WSMsgType.TEXT:
                # Handle incoming messages
                pass
            elif msg.type == web.WSMsgType.CLOSE:
                break
    except Exception as e:
        print(f"Connection error: {e}")
    finally:
        clients.remove(ws)
        await ws.close()
```

In this example:

- We include exception handling around the message loop to catch connection errors and clean up appropriately.

4. Testing Multiple Connections

To ensure your WebSocket server handles multiple connections effectively, conduct testing with multiple clients. You can use different browser tabs or tools like WebSocket testing clients to simulate multiple users connecting to the server.

Start the WebSocket Server: Run your websocket_server.py script.

Open Multiple Clients: Open several browser tabs pointing to the HTML dashboard (or create multiple instances of the client you developed).

Send Messages: Test sending messages from different clients and ensure that all clients receive the broadcasted messages.

Monitor Connections: Monitor the server logs to observe connections and disconnections, ensuring that the server handles them appropriately.

In this section, we successfully explored how to handle multiple Web-Socket connections using the aiohttp library. By managing connected clients, broadcasting messages, and implementing strategies for high concurrency, we have built a robust framework for real-time communication.

Implementing Client-Side WebSocket Logic

In this section, we will focus on implementing the client-side logic for interacting with the WebSocket server. This includes establishing a WebSocket connection, sending messages, receiving data from the server, and updating the user interface accordingly. We will also discuss error handling and best practices for maintaining a responsive and interactive client application.

1. Setting Up the Client-Side HTML Structure

First, create an HTML file (e.g., client_dashboard.html) to serve as the user interface for your WebSocket client. This dashboard will include an input field for sending messages and a display area for incoming messages.

Example HTML Structure:

html

```html
<!DOCTYPE html>
<html lang="en">
<head>
    <meta charset="UTF-8">
    <meta name="viewport" content="width=device-width,
    initial-scale=1.0">
    <title>WebSocket Client Dashboard</title>
    <style>
        body {
            font-family: Arial, sans-serif;
            margin: 0;
            padding: 20px;
            background-color: #f4f4f4;
        }
        #data-container {
            margin-top: 20px;
        }
        .data-item {
            padding: 10px;
            border: 1px solid #ccc;
            margin-bottom: 10px;
            border-radius: 5px;
            background-color: #fff;
        }
    </style>
</head>
<body>
    <h1>WebSocket Client Dashboard</h1>
    <input type="text" id="messageInput" placeholder="Type your
    message..." autocomplete="off">
    <button id="sendButton">Send</button>
    <div id="data-container"></div>

    <script src="client_logic.js"></script>
</body>
</html>
```

In this HTML structure:

- We have a text input for the user to type messages and a button to send them.
- A div container (data-container) is included to display incoming messages from the server.

2. Implementing the Client-Side WebSocket Logic

Now, let's create a JavaScript file (client_logic.js) that will handle the WebSocket communication and user interactions.

Establishing the WebSocket Connection

The first step is to create a WebSocket connection to the server. This involves setting up event listeners to handle connection open, message receipt, and connection close events.

Example of Connecting to the WebSocket Server:

javascript

```
const ws = new WebSocket('ws://localhost:8080/ws');  // Connect
to the WebSocket server
const messageInput = document.getElementById('messageInput');
const sendButton = document.getElementById('sendButton');
const dataContainer = document.getElementById('data-container');

ws.onopen = function() {
    console.log('Connected to the WebSocket server.');
};

ws.onclose = function() {
    console.log('Disconnected from the WebSocket server.');
};

ws.onerror = function(error) {
    console.error('WebSocket error:', error);
};
```

In this code:

- We create a new WebSocket object and specify the server URL.
- We log connection events for monitoring purposes.

Sending Messages

Next, we will implement the functionality for sending messages to the server. This will involve capturing the input from the text field and sending it over the WebSocket connection when the user clicks the send button.

Example of Sending Messages:

```javascript
sendButton.onclick = function() {
    const message = messageInput.value;
    if (message) {
        ws.send(message);  // Send the message to the server
        messageInput.value = '';  // Clear the input field
    }
};

// Allow sending messages by pressing the Enter key
messageInput.addEventListener('keypress', function(event) {
    if (event.key === 'Enter') {
        sendButton.click();  // Trigger click event on the send
        button
    }
});
```

In this implementation:

- When the send button is clicked, the message from the input field is sent to the server.
- The input field is cleared after sending the message.
- An event listener is added to allow sending messages by pressing the Enter key.

Receiving and Displaying Messages

We need to implement the logic for receiving messages from the server and displaying them in the data container. This will create a dynamic experience for users as they see messages arrive in real time.

Example of Receiving Messages:

```javascript
ws.onmessage = function(event) {
    const data = JSON.parse(event.data);  // Parse the incoming
    message
    const dataItem = document.createElement('div');
    dataItem.className = 'data-item';
    dataItem.textContent = `Sensor ID: ${data.sensor_id}, Value:
    ${data.value.toFixed(2)}`;  // Display the data
    dataContainer.appendChild(dataItem);  // Append the data item
    to the container
};
```

In this code:

- We handle incoming messages using the onmessage event listener.
- Each message is parsed, and the relevant data is displayed as a new div element in the data container.

3. Handling Connection State and Errors

Properly managing the connection state and handling errors is essential for providing a robust user experience. We can enhance our client-side logic by adding notifications for connection status and handling WebSocket errors gracefully.

Example of Enhanced Connection Handling:

```javascript
ws.onopen = function() {
    console.log('Connected to the WebSocket server.');
```

```
     // Optionally update the UI to indicate connection status
     dataContainer.innerHTML += '<div class="data-item">Connected
     to the server.</div>';
 };

 ws.onclose = function() {
     console.log('Disconnected from the WebSocket server.');
     // Update the UI to indicate disconnection
     dataContainer.innerHTML += '<div
     class="data-item">Disconnected from the server.</div>';
 };

 ws.onerror = function(error) {
     console.error('WebSocket error:', error);
     // Optionally display an error message to the user
     dataContainer.innerHTML += `<div class="data-item">Error:
     ${error.message}</div>`;
 };
```

In this enhanced example:

- We provide user feedback for connection events and errors by updating the UI to reflect the connection state.
- Errors are logged to the console and displayed in the UI for better user awareness.

4. Testing the Client-Side WebSocket Logic

Once you have implemented the client-side logic, you can test the functionality:

Start the WebSocket Server: Ensure your WebSocket server is running.

Open the Client Dashboard: Open the client_dashboard.html file in your web browser.

Test Sending and Receiving Messages: Type messages in the input field and send them. Observe how they are received and displayed in the data container.

Test Multiple Clients: Open multiple instances of the client dashboard in different tabs or windows to test message broadcasting between clients.

In this section, we successfully implemented the client-side WebSocket logic for our real-time data dashboard. By establishing a WebSocket connection, handling user inputs, and dynamically updating the UI with incoming messages, we have created an interactive and responsive application.

The concepts covered here provide a solid foundation for building more sophisticated applications that leverage real-time data processing with WebSockets.

Integrating Asynchronous Programming with APIs

Building a RESTful API with FastAPI
FastAPI is a modern, fast (high-performance) web framework for building APIs with Python 3.6+ based on standard Python type hints. It is designed to create RESTful APIs quickly and efficiently, making use of asynchronous programming to handle requests. FastAPI simplifies the process of building APIs by providing automatic validation, serialization, and documentation while fully supporting asynchronous programming. In this chapter, we will explore how to build a RESTful API using FastAPI, focusing on its key features, installation, and practical implementation.

1. Overview of FastAPI

FastAPI is designed with performance and ease of use in mind. Some of its standout features include:

- **Asynchronous Support**: FastAPI fully supports asynchronous programming, allowing you to define asynchronous routes and handle high levels of concurrency effectively.
- **Automatic Data Validation**: FastAPI uses Pydantic for data validation, enabling automatic request body validation and response serialization based on defined models.
- **Interactive Documentation**: FastAPI automatically generates OpenAPI and Swagger documentation for your API, making it easy for

developers to understand and test the API endpoints.

- **Type Safety**: By utilizing Python type hints, FastAPI provides type safety, improving code clarity and reducing bugs.

2. Installing FastAPI and Uvicorn

To get started with FastAPI, you need to install the framework along with an ASGI server. Uvicorn is a popular choice for running FastAPI applications.

Installation Steps:

Create a new directory for your project:

```bash

mkdir fastapi_project
cd fastapi_project
```

Create and activate a virtual environment:

```bash

python -m venv venv
source venv/bin/activate  # On
Windows use venv\Scripts\activate
```

Install FastAPI and Uvicorn:

```bash

pip install fastapi uvicorn
```

3. Creating Your First FastAPI Application

Now that you have FastAPI installed, you can create your first API application. Let's start with a simple example that demonstrates the key components of a FastAPI application.

Basic FastAPI Application

Create a new Python file (e.g., main.py) and add the following code:

```python
from fastapi import FastAPI

app = FastAPI()  # Create an instance of
 the FastAPI application

@app.get("/")  # Define a GET endpoint
async def read_root():
    return {"message": "Welcome to FastAPI!"}

@app.get("/items/{item_id}")  # Define a dynamic route
async def read_item(item_id: int, q: str = None):
    return {"item_id": item_id, "query": q}
```

In this code:

- We import FastAPI and create an instance of it.
- We define two endpoints:
- A root endpoint that returns a welcome message.
- An endpoint that retrieves an item based on the item_id path parameter and an optional query parameter q.

Running the Application

You can run the FastAPI application using Uvicorn. In the terminal, execute the following command:

```bash
uvicorn main:app --reload
```

- main refers to the name of your Python file (excluding the .py extension).
- app is the instance of the FastAPI application.

- The —reload option enables auto-reloading for development, allowing changes to be reflected without restarting the server.

You should see output indicating that the server is running. By default, it listens on http://127.0.0.1:8000.

4. Accessing the API

With the server running, you can access your API:

Open your web browser and navigate to http://127.0.0.1:8000/. You should see the JSON response:

```json
{
    "message": "Welcome to FastAPI!"
}
```

To access the dynamic route, go to http://127.0.0.1:8000/items/1?q=test. The response will look like this:

```json
{
    "item_id": 1,
    "query": "test"
}
```

FastAPI automatically generates interactive API documentation. You can access it by navigating to http://127.0.0.1:8000/docs, which provides a Swagger UI for testing your API endpoints.

5. Defining Data Models with Pydantic

FastAPI uses Pydantic for data validation and serialization. You can define data models that specify the structure of your request and response bodies.

Creating a Data Model

Let's define a simple data model for an item:

```python
from pydantic import BaseModel

class Item(BaseModel):
    id: int
    name: str
    description: str = None  # Optional field
    price: float
```

In this code:

- We create a data model Item that extends BaseModel from Pydantic.
- We define the fields with types, and specify optional fields with default values.

Using the Data Model in API Endpoints

You can now use this data model in your API endpoints to validate request bodies.

Example of Using the Item Model:

```python
@app.post("/items/")
async def create_item(item: Item):
    return {"item_id": item.id, "name": item.name, "price":
    item.price}
```

In this example:

- We define a POST endpoint that expects a request body conforming to the Item model.
- FastAPI automatically validates the incoming data and converts it to an instance of Item.

6. Handling Query Parameters and Path Parameters

FastAPI allows you to define both query parameters and path parameters easily.

Defining Query Parameters

Query parameters can be added to your route definitions directly as function arguments.

Example of Query Parameters:

python

```python
@app.get("/items/")
async def get_items(skip: int = 0, limit: int = 10):
    return {"skip": skip, "limit": limit}
```

In this example:

- The skip and limit parameters are optional query parameters with default values.
- You can access this endpoint using a URL like http://127.0.0.1:8000/items/?skip=5&limit=15.

Using Path Parameters

Path parameters are defined by including them in the route string.

Example of Path Parameters:

python

```python
@app.get("/users/{user_id}")
async def get_user(user_id: int):
    return {"user_id": user_id}
```

In this case:

- The endpoint accepts a path parameter user_id, which is an integer.

7. Error Handling in FastAPI

FastAPI provides built-in error handling for validation errors and allows you to define custom error responses.

Automatic Error Handling

If the incoming request data does not conform to the defined data model, FastAPI will automatically return a 422 Unprocessable Entity error with a descriptive message.

Custom Error Handling

You can create custom exception handlers to handle specific exceptions and return custom responses.

Example of Custom Error Handling:

```python
from fastapi import HTTPException

@app.get("/items/{item_id}")
async def get_item(item_id: int):
    if item_id not in available_items:
        raise HTTPException(status_code=404,
 detail="Item not found")
    return {"item_id": item_id}
```

In this code:

- If an invalid item_id is requested, a HTTPException is raised, which FastAPI handles by returning a 404 error with a custom message.

In this chapter, we explored how to build a RESTful API using FastAPI, focusing on its asynchronous capabilities, data modeling with Pydantic, and error handling. By leveraging FastAPI's features, you can quickly create high-performance APIs that support real-time data processing and handle multiple connections efficiently.

Authentication and Security Considerations

When building web applications, especially those that expose APIs, implementing robust authentication and security measures is essential. This section will explore various authentication strategies in FastAPI, including OAuth2, JWT (JSON Web Tokens), and basic authentication. Additionally, we will cover best practices for securing your FastAPI application against common vulnerabilities.

1. Understanding Authentication in FastAPI

FastAPI provides built-in support for various authentication methods. The framework allows developers to implement authentication mechanisms that suit their application requirements.

Authentication Strategies

Here are some common authentication strategies that you can implement in your FastAPI applications:

- **Basic Authentication**: A simple method where users provide a username and password, which are sent in an HTTP header. This method is not very secure unless used over HTTPS.
- **OAuth2**: A more robust authentication framework commonly used for third-party authentication. It allows applications to obtain limited access to user accounts on an HTTP service, such as Google, Facebook, or GitHub.
- **JWT (JSON Web Tokens)**: A compact, URL-safe means of representing claims to be transferred between two parties. JWT is often used for stateless authentication in web applications.

2. Implementing OAuth2 with FastAPI

OAuth2 is one of the most common authentication methods for APIs. FastAPI makes it easy to implement OAuth2 with password flow and token-based authentication.

Setting Up OAuth2 Password Flow

To implement OAuth2, you need to install the passlib library for password hashing:

```bash
bash
```

```bash
pip install passlib[bcrypt]
```

Next, you can create a simple user model, a fake user database, and implement OAuth2 authentication.

Example Implementation:

```python
python
```

```python
from fastapi import FastAPI, Depends, HTTPException, status
from fastapi.security import OAuth2PasswordBearer,
OAuth2PasswordRequestForm
from passlib.context import CryptContext

app = FastAPI()

# User model
class User:
    def __init__(self, username: str,
 full_name: str = None, email: str = None):
        self.username = username
        self.full_name = full_name
        self.email = email

# Fake user database
fake_users_db = {
    "johndoe": {
        "username": "johndoe",
        "full_name": "John Doe",
        "email": "johndoe@example.com",
        "hashed_password":
"$2b$12$KIXM8A.
1zwBPUcB7sOeDKeK
```

```
5tY38EXpM6Zn
HR9SK1dAzJ1Aeb3h8K",
# bcrypt hash for "secret"
        "disabled": False,
    }
}


# Password hashing
pwd_context = CryptContext(schemes=["bcrypt"], deprecated="auto")
oauth2_scheme = OAuth2PasswordBearer(tokenUrl="token")

def verify_password(plain_password, hashed_password):
    return pwd_context.verify(plain_password, hashed_password)

def get_user(db, username: str):
    if username in db:
        user_dict = db[username]
        return User(**user_dict)

def authenticate_user(db, username: str, password: str):
    user = get_user(db, username)
    if user is None or not verify_password(password,
    user.hashed_password):
        return False
    return user

@app.post("/token")
async def login(form_data:
OAuth2PasswordRequestForm = Depends()):
    user = authenticate_user
(fake_users_db, form_data.username, form_data.password)
    if not user:
        raise HTTPException(
            status_code=status.HTTP_401_UNAUTHORIZED,
            detail="Incorrect username or password",
            headers={"WWW-Authenticate": "Bearer"},
        )
    return {"access_token": user.username,
  "token_type": "bearer"}
```

```
@app.get("/users/me")
async def read_users_me(token: str = Depends(oauth2_scheme)):
    # Here, you'd typically decode the token and retrieve user
    information.
    return {"token": token}
```

In this code:

- We define a user model and a fake user database with hashed passwords.
- We create functions to verify passwords and authenticate users.
- The /token endpoint is implemented for logging in and returning a bearer token.

Testing the OAuth2 Implementation

Start the FastAPI server.

Use an HTTP client (like Postman or CURL) to send a POST request to /token with the form data containing username and password:

```bash
POST /token
Content-Type: application/x-www-form-urlencoded

username=johndoe&password=secret
```

If the credentials are correct, you will receive a response with an access token.

Use the access token to access the protected route:

```vbnet
GET /users/me
Authorization: Bearer <access_token>
```

3. Securing Your FastAPI Application

When building an API, it's essential to incorporate security best practices to protect against common vulnerabilities.

Use HTTPS

Always serve your application over HTTPS to encrypt data in transit. This prevents eavesdropping and man-in-the-middle attacks. If deploying to production, consider using services like Let's Encrypt to obtain free SSL certificates.

Implement Rate Limiting

To prevent abuse of your API, implement rate limiting to restrict the number of requests a user can make in a given time frame. You can use libraries like slowapi to add rate limiting to FastAPI.

Example of Rate Limiting with SlowAPI:

```bash
pip install slowapi
```

```python
from slowapi import Limiter
from slowapi.errors import RateLimitExceeded

limiter = Limiter(key_func=get_remote_address)

@app.exception_handler(RateLimitExceeded)
async def rate_limit_exceeded(request, exc):
    return JSONResponse(
        status_code=HTTP_429_TOO_MANY_REQUESTS,
        content={"detail": "Too many requests"},
    )

@app.get("/rate-limited")
@limiter.limit("5/minute")
async def rate_limited_endpoint():
    return {"message": "This endpoint is rate limited."}
```

In this example, we apply a rate limit of 5 requests per minute to the /rate-limited endpoint.

Validate Input Data

Always validate and sanitize input data to protect against SQL injection, XSS, and other attacks. FastAPI's Pydantic models automatically handle data validation, ensuring that the data received is in the expected format.

Use CORS Wisely

Cross-Origin Resource Sharing (CORS) allows or restricts resources on a web page to be requested from another domain. Use FastAPI's built-in CORS middleware to control which origins are allowed to access your API.

Example of Setting Up CORS:

```bash
pip install fastapi[all]
python
```

```python
from fastapi.middleware.cors import CORSMiddleware

app.add_middleware(
    CORSMiddleware,
    allow_origins=["http://localhost:3000"],  # Adjust as
    necessary
    allow_credentials=True,
    allow_methods=["*"],
    allow_headers=["*"],
)
```

In this code, we configure CORS to allow requests from specific origins, enhancing security.

Logging and Monitoring

Implement logging to keep track of access patterns, errors, and anomalies. This information can help you monitor the security of your application and detect potential threats. Use logging libraries such as Python's built-in logging module or third-party services like Sentry for monitoring.

In this section, we explored how to implement authentication in FastAPI using OAuth2, covering both the password flow and token-based authentication. We also discussed important security considerations, including using HTTPS, rate limiting, input validation, and configuring CORS.

Integrating Third-Party APIs Asynchronously

Integrating third-party APIs is a common requirement in modern applications, allowing developers to enhance functionality by leveraging external services such as payment processors, data providers, social media platforms, and more. When working with asynchronous programming in Python, particularly with FastAPI, you can efficiently manage these integrations without blocking your application's responsiveness. In this section, we will explore how to make asynchronous calls to third-party APIs, handle the responses, and implement best practices for error handling and performance optimization.

1. Understanding Asynchronous API Calls

Asynchronous API calls allow your application to send requests to external services without blocking the main execution thread. This means that while waiting for the external service to respond, your application can continue processing other tasks, which is especially important for high-performance applications that require real-time interactions.

Benefits of Asynchronous API Calls

- **Non-Blocking Operations**: Free up resources while waiting for responses, enhancing the responsiveness of your application.
- **Improved Performance**: Handle multiple requests simultaneously, making better use of network I/O and reducing latency.
- **Scalability**: Handle more concurrent connections, which is vital for applications with many users.

2. Making Asynchronous API Calls with httpx

To make asynchronous HTTP requests in FastAPI, you can use the httpx library, which supports both synchronous and asynchronous requests. First, you need to install httpx:

```bash
pip install httpx
```

Example of Making Asynchronous API Calls

Here's how to use httpx to make an asynchronous GET request to a third-party API. For demonstration purposes, we will use the JSONPlaceholder API, which is a free fake online REST API for testing and prototyping.

Example Implementation:

```python
import httpx
from fastapi import FastAPI

app = FastAPI()

@app.get("/posts/{post_id}")
async def get_post(post_id: int):
    async with httpx.AsyncClient() as client:
        response = await client.get
(f"https://jsonplaceholder.
typicode.com/posts/{post_id}")
        response.raise_for_status()  # Raise an error for bad
        responses
        return response.json()  # Return the JSON response
```

In this example:

- We create a GET endpoint /posts/{post_id} that takes a post ID as a path parameter.
- Using httpx.AsyncClient, we make an asynchronous GET request to the JSONPlaceholder API.

- We handle potential errors by calling response.raise_for_status(), which raises an exception for HTTP error responses.

3. Handling API Responses

When integrating third-party APIs, it's essential to handle responses appropriately, including success, failure, and edge cases.

Handling Successful Responses

Typically, a successful API call will return a 200 OK status with the requested data. You can directly return this data to the client or process it further as needed.

Example of Handling a Successful Response:

python

```
@app.get("/comments/{post_id}")
async def get_comments(post_id: int):
    async with httpx.AsyncClient() as client:
        response = await client.get
(f"https://jsonplaceholder.
typicode.com/posts/
{post_id}/comments")
        response.raise_for_status()
# Raise error for non-2xx responses
        return response.json()
# Return comments related to the post
```

Handling Errors

You should handle possible errors gracefully, including client errors (4xx), server errors (5xx), and connection timeouts.

Example of Error Handling:

python

```
@app.get("/user/{user_id}")
async def get_user(user_id: int):
    async with httpx.AsyncClient() as client:
```

```
       try:
            response = await client.
get(f"https://jsonplaceholder.
typicode.com/users/{user_id}")
            response.raise_for_status()
 # Raise error for non-2xx responses
            return response.json()
        except httpx.HTTPStatusError as e:
            return {"error": f"User not found:
            {e.response.status_code}"}
        except httpx.RequestError as e:
            return {"error": f"An error
occurred while requesting: {str(e)}"}
```

In this code:

- We catch HTTPStatusError for non-200 responses and RequestError for issues related to the request itself, providing clear error messages to the client.

4. Best Practices for Integrating Third-Party APIs

To ensure efficient and reliable integration with third-party APIs, consider the following best practices:

Use Timeouts

Set timeouts for your API requests to prevent your application from hanging indefinitely if the external service is unresponsive.

Example of Setting Timeouts:

python

```
async with httpx.AsyncClient(timeout=10.0)
as client:  # 10 seconds timeout
    response = await client.get(url)
```

Rate Limiting

Be mindful of rate limits imposed by third-party APIs. Implement logic to handle rate limiting, such as exponential backoff strategies or queuing requests to avoid exceeding the limit.

Caching Responses

For APIs that return data that does not change frequently, consider caching responses to minimize the number of API calls and reduce latency. Libraries like diskcache or cachetools can help manage caching efficiently.

Logging API Interactions

Log API requests and responses for monitoring and debugging purposes. This information can help you diagnose issues with the API or identify performance bottlenecks.

Example of Logging Requests:

```python
import logging

logging.basicConfig(level=logging.INFO)

@app.get("/data/{item_id}")
async def get_data(item_id: int):
    logging.info(f"Fetching data for item_id: {item_id}")
    async with httpx.AsyncClient() as client:
        response = await
        client.get(f"https://api.example.com/data/{item_id}")
        response.raise_for_status()
        return response.json()
```

Secure Sensitive Data

When dealing with sensitive data, such as API keys or user credentials, ensure that this information is stored securely and not exposed in logs or error messages.

In this section, we explored how to integrate third-party APIs asynchronously in FastAPI using the httpx library. By making asynchronous requests, handling responses, and implementing best practices, you can create efficient and reliable integrations with external services.

Rate Limiting and Caching Strategies

When building APIs, especially those that are publicly accessible or used heavily, implementing rate limiting and caching strategies is crucial for maintaining performance, reliability, and security. Rate limiting helps control the number of requests a user can make in a specific time frame, while caching improves response times and reduces the load on the server and the external services. This section will cover the concepts, implementations, and best practices for both rate limiting and caching in FastAPI.

1. Rate Limiting

Rate limiting is a technique used to control the amount of incoming requests to your API over a specific time period. This helps to prevent abuse, ensure fair use among users, and protect backend services from being overwhelmed.

Why Implement Rate Limiting?

- **Prevent Abuse**: Rate limiting protects your API from malicious attacks such as DDoS (Distributed Denial of Service) attacks.
- **Fair Usage**: Ensures that all users have equitable access to the API, preventing any single user from monopolizing resources.
- **Resource Management**: Helps in managing load on the server and backend services, allowing for better performance and reliability.

Implementing Rate Limiting in FastAPI

To implement rate limiting in FastAPI, you can use the slowapi library, which provides easy-to-use decorators for rate limiting.

Installation:

```bash
pip install slowapi
```

173

Basic Implementation Example:

Here's how to set up rate limiting using slowapi:

```python
from fastapi import FastAPI, Depends
from slowapi import Limiter
from slowapi.errors import RateLimitExceeded
from fastapi.responses import JSONResponse

app = FastAPI()
limiter = Limiter
(key_func=lambda: "global")
 # You can customize the key function
for user-specific limits

@app.exception_handler(RateLimitExceeded)
async def rate_limit_exceeded(request, exc):
    return JSONResponse(
        status_code=429,
        content={"detail": "Too many requests, please try again
        later."},
    )

@app.get("/limited-endpoint")
@limiter.limit("5/minute")  # Limit to 5 requests per minute
async def limited_endpoint():
    return {"message": "This endpoint is rate limited."}
```

In this example:

- We create an instance of Limiter and set a global rate limit.
- The /limited-endpoint route is limited to 5 requests per minute. If a user exceeds this limit, a 429 error is returned.

User-Specific Rate Limits

To set up user-specific rate limits, you can modify the key_func to differentiate between users based on their IP address or any user-specific identifier.

```python

from slowapi.util import get_remote_address

limiter = Limiter(key_func=get_remote_address)
 # Rate limits based on user IP
```

This configuration ensures that each user has their own rate limit, providing fair usage across the API.

Caching Strategies

Caching is the process of storing frequently accessed data in a temporary storage area to reduce the time taken to retrieve that data. Caching can significantly improve the performance of your API by reducing latency and load on your backend services.

Why Implement Caching?

- **Performance Improvement**: Cached responses can be served much faster than querying the database or making an API call.
- **Reduced Load**: Decreases the number of requests to the database or external APIs, leading to lower operational costs.
- **Scalability**: Helps your application handle more users and requests simultaneously.

Types of Caching

In-Memory Caching: Fastest access time, suitable for frequently accessed data that doesn't require persistence. Libraries like cachetools or diskcache can be used for in-memory caching.

Distributed Caching: Used for large-scale applications, allowing multiple instances of the application to share a common cache. Redis and Memcached are popular choices for distributed caching.

HTTP Caching: Leverages HTTP headers (like Cache-Control, ETag, etc.) to allow browsers and intermediate proxies to cache responses.

Implementing Caching in FastAPI

To implement in-memory caching using cachetools, you can set it up as follows:

Installation:

```bash
pip install cachetools
```

Example of In-Memory Caching:

```python
from fastapi import FastAPI
from cachetools import TTLCache, cached

app = FastAPI()
cache = TTLCache(maxsize=100, ttl=300)
# Cache with a max size and a
time-to-live of 300 seconds

@cached(cache)
@app.get("/data/{item_id}")
async def get_data(item_id: int):
    # Simulate a slow data retrieval operation
    await asyncio.sleep(2)  # Simulate delay
    return {"item_id":
item_id, "value":
f"Data for item {item_id}"}
```

In this code:

- We create a TTL cache that stores up to 100 items and expires entries after 300 seconds.
- The @cached decorator automatically caches the results of the get_data

function based on its arguments.

Implementing HTTP Caching

For HTTP caching, you can add caching headers to your responses. FastAPI makes it easy to set custom headers in your responses.

Example of Setting HTTP Caching Headers:

```python
from fastapi import FastAPI, Response

app = FastAPI()

@app.get("/cacheable-data")
async def cacheable_data(response: Response):
    response.headers["Cache-Control"] =
"public, max-age=3600"  # Cache for 1 hour
    return {"message": "This data can be cached."}
```

In this example, the Cache-Control header instructs clients to cache the response for one hour.

3. Best Practices for Rate Limiting and Caching

To effectively implement rate limiting and caching in your API, consider the following best practices:

Monitor Usage Patterns

Regularly analyze logs and metrics to understand usage patterns. This will help you adjust rate limits and caching strategies based on actual user behavior.

Set Appropriate Limits

When implementing rate limits, consider the nature of your API and the expected usage patterns. Adjust limits based on user roles, API endpoints, or user-specific requirements.

Cache Wisely

Choose what data to cache carefully. Cache data that is frequently accessed but does not change often. Avoid caching sensitive or user-specific information.

Invalidate Cache Appropriately

Ensure you have a strategy for cache invalidation when underlying data changes. This can be done through time-to-live settings, manual invalidation, or event-driven invalidation.

Test Your Implementation

Thoroughly test your rate limiting and caching implementations under load to ensure they perform as expected without negatively impacting the user experience.

In this section, we covered the importance of rate limiting and caching in building robust and scalable APIs with FastAPI. By implementing these strategies, you can protect your API from abuse, improve response times, and reduce the load on your backend services.

Deploying Your API

Deploying a FastAPI application is a critical step in making your API available for production use. Proper deployment ensures that your API is reliable, scalable, and secure. In this section, we will explore various methods for deploying your FastAPI application, including using Uvicorn, Docker, cloud platforms, and more. We will also cover best practices for maintaining and monitoring your deployed API.

1. Preparing for Deployment

Before deploying your FastAPI application, consider the following preparatory steps:

Environment Configuration

Ensure that your application is configured to run in a production environment. This includes:

- Setting environment variables for sensitive information (e.g., database

URLs, API keys).
- Using a configuration management library like pydantic or python-dotenv to manage environment-specific settings.

Dependency Management

Make sure you have a requirements.txt file that lists all dependencies for your project. You can generate this file using:

```bash
pip freeze > requirements.txt
```

This file can be used to recreate your environment on the server.

2. Running FastAPI with Uvicorn

Uvicorn is a lightning-fast ASGI server that is ideal for running FastAPI applications. In a production environment, it is common to run Uvicorn behind a reverse proxy like Nginx.

Running Uvicorn

You can run your FastAPI application using the following command:

```bash
uvicorn main:app --host 0.0.0.0
  --port 8000 --workers 4
```

- main:app refers to the FastAPI application instance.
- —host 0.0.0.0 allows the server to be accessible from any IP address.
- —port 8000 specifies the port to listen on.
- —workers 4 runs multiple worker processes to handle concurrent requests.

This command will work for testing and development but is not recommended for production without a reverse proxy.

Using Gunicorn with Uvicorn Workers

For production, it is recommended to use Gunicorn with Uvicorn workers to take advantage of process management.

Installation:

```bash
```

```bash
pip install gunicorn[uvicorn]
```

Running the Application:

You can run the application using Gunicorn with Uvicorn workers like this:

```bash
```

```bash
gunicorn main:app -w 4 -k uvicorn.
workers.UvicornWorker --bind 0.0.0.0:8000
```

- -w 4 specifies the number of worker processes.
- -k uvicorn.workers.UvicornWorker tells Gunicorn to use Uvicorn workers for handling requests.

3. Deploying with Docker

Docker is a popular tool for containerizing applications, ensuring consistent environments across development and production. Here's how to deploy your FastAPI application using Docker.

Creating a Dockerfile

Create a Dockerfile in your project directory:

```dockerfile
```

```
# Use the official Python image from the Docker Hub
FROM python:3.9-slim

# Set the working directory in the container
WORKDIR /app

# Copy the requirements file and install dependencies
COPY requirements.txt .
RUN pip install --no-cache-dir -r requirements.txt

# Copy the application code into the container
COPY . .

# Command to run the application
CMD ["uvicorn", "main:app", "--host",
 "0.0.0.0", "--port", "8000"]
```

Building and Running the Docker Container

To build and run your Docker container, use the following commands:

```bash
bash

# Build the Docker image
docker build -t fastapi-app .

# Run the Docker container
docker run -d -p 8000:8000 fastapi-app
```

- The -d flag runs the container in detached mode.
- The -p 8000:8000 option maps port 8000 on your host to port 8000 in the container.

4. Deploying to Cloud Platforms

You can deploy your FastAPI application to various cloud platforms. Here are some popular options:

Heroku

Heroku is a platform-as-a-service (PaaS) that makes it easy to deploy applications. To deploy your FastAPI app to Heroku:

Install the Heroku CLI and log in.

Create a Procfile in your project directory:

bash

```
web: gunicorn main:app -w 4 -k
uvicorn.workers.UvicornWorker
--bind 0.0.0.0:${PORT}
```

Initialize a Git repository, commit your changes, and deploy to Heroku:

bash

```
git init
heroku create your-app-name
git add .
git commit -m "Initial commit"
git push heroku master
```

Your application will be accessible at https://your-app-name.herokuapp.com.

AWS Elastic Beanstalk

AWS Elastic Beanstalk is another option for deploying FastAPI applications. Here's a high-level overview:

Package your application and dependencies.

Create a new Elastic Beanstalk environment with a Python platform.

Upload your application package.

Elastic Beanstalk handles provisioning, load balancing, and scaling.

Google Cloud Run

Google Cloud Run is a serverless platform for running containers. To deploy using Cloud Run:

Install the Google Cloud SDK.

Build your Docker image and push it to Google Container Registry:

bash

```
gcloud builds submit --tag gcr.
io/your-project-id/fastapi-app
```

Deploy the container to Cloud Run:

bash

```
gcloud run deploy --image gcr.
io/your-project-id/fastapi-app --platform managed
```

5. Securing Your Deployment

Once your FastAPI application is deployed, it's important to secure it:

- **Use HTTPS**: Ensure your application is served over HTTPS to encrypt data in transit.
- **Environment Variables**: Store sensitive data like API keys and database URLs in environment variables rather than hard-coding them in your application.
- **Regular Updates**: Keep your dependencies and environment updated to mitigate vulnerabilities.
- **Monitoring and Logging**: Implement monitoring and logging to track performance and security incidents.

In this section, we covered the deployment of FastAPI applications, including local deployments using Uvicorn and Gunicorn, containerization with Docker, and deploying to cloud platforms like Heroku, AWS Elastic Beanstalk, and Google Cloud Run. We also discussed best practices for securing your deployment to ensure that your API remains reliable and secure in a production environment.

Optimizing Performance in Asynchronous Applications

P**rofiling and Measuring Performance**
Optimizing the performance of asynchronous applications is crucial for ensuring they can handle high loads, deliver quick responses, and provide a seamless user experience. To effectively optimize performance, developers must first understand how to profile and measure their applications. Profiling helps identify bottlenecks and areas for improvement, while performance measurement provides insights into how the application behaves under various conditions. In this chapter, we will explore the methods and tools for profiling and measuring performance in asynchronous applications, particularly in the context of Python and frameworks like FastAPI.

1. Understanding Profiling

Profiling is the process of measuring the performance of an application to identify parts of the code that consume the most resources, such as CPU time, memory usage, or I/O operations. Profiling provides detailed insights that enable developers to make informed decisions about where to optimize their applications.

Types of Profiling

CPU Profiling: Measures how much CPU time each function consumes. This type of profiling is crucial for identifying inefficient algorithms or bottlenecks in the execution flow.

Memory Profiling: Tracks memory allocation and usage throughout the application's execution. Memory leaks and excessive memory consumption can lead to performance degradation.

I/O Profiling: Monitors input/output operations, such as file reading/writing and network requests. This is especially important for asynchronous applications, where I/O-bound operations can introduce latency.

2. Tools for Profiling in Python

Several tools are available for profiling Python applications, including built-in modules and third-party libraries. Below are some popular profiling tools that you can use for your asynchronous applications.

cProfile

cProfile is a built-in Python module that provides a straightforward way to profile your application.

Example of Using cProfile:

```python
import cProfile
import asyncio

async def slow_function():
    await asyncio.sleep(1)
    return "Finished"

async def main():
    tasks = [slow_function() for _ in range(10)]
    await asyncio.gather(*tasks)

# Profile the main function
cProfile.run("asyncio.run(main())")
```

This code will produce a report showing how much time was spent in each function, allowing you to identify bottlenecks.

Py-Spy

py-spy is a sampling profiler for Python applications. It can profile running Python programs without modifying their source code. It generates flame graphs that visualize where the program spends most of its time.

Installation:

```bash
pip install py-spy
```

Usage:

You can run py-spy as follows:

```bash
py-spy top --pid <PID>
```

Replace <PID> with the process ID of your running application. This will provide a live view of function calls and their CPU usage.

Memory Profiler

memory_profiler is a module for monitoring memory usage in Python programs. It provides line-by-line memory usage statistics.

Installation:

```bash
pip install memory_profiler
```

Usage:

To profile memory usage, decorate your functions with @profile and run your script with the -m memory_profiler option.

```python
```

```
@profile
def my_function():
    # Your code here
```

This will output the memory usage for each line when the function is executed.

3. Measuring Performance

In addition to profiling, it's essential to measure the performance of your application to understand how it behaves under load. This involves monitoring response times, throughput, and resource usage.

Response Time Measurement

Response time is the time taken to process a request and return a response. You can measure response times by adding logging to your FastAPI routes.

Example of Measuring Response Time in FastAPI:

```python
import time
from fastapi import FastAPI, Request

app = FastAPI()

@app.middleware("http")
async def measure_time(request: Request, call_next):
    start_time = time.time()
    response = await call_next(request)
    duration = time.time() - start_time
    response.headers["X-Response-Time"] = str(duration)
    return response
```

This middleware logs the duration it takes to process each request and adds it to the response headers.

Throughput Measurement

Throughput measures the number of requests handled by the application over a specific time frame. You can use load testing tools to simulate concurrent users and measure throughput.

Load Testing Tools:

Locust: A scalable load testing tool that allows you to define user behavior in Python.

Apache JMeter: A widely-used Java-based tool for performance testing that can be used to create test plans for HTTP requests.

Artillery: A modern, powerful, and easy-to-use load testing toolkit for HTTP and WebSocket APIs.

Example of Using Locust:

Install Locust:

```bash
pip install locust
```

Create a locustfile.py:

```python
from locust import HttpUser, task, between

class APIUser(HttpUser):
    wait_time = between(1, 5)

    @task
    def get_posts(self):
        self.client.get("/posts/1")  # Adjust the endpoint as
        necessary
```

Run Locust:

```bash
```

```
locust -f locustfile.py --host=http://127.0.0.1:8000
```

Open your browser and navigate to http://localhost:8089 to start the load test.

4. Optimizing Performance Based on Profiling Results

Once you have gathered profiling and performance measurement data, you can analyze it to identify areas for optimization. Here are some common strategies:

Optimize Slow Functions

Identify functions with high CPU usage and optimize them by:

- Refactoring to improve algorithm efficiency.
- Caching results of expensive computations.
- Offloading tasks to background jobs if they can be processed asynchronously.

Reduce Memory Usage

Monitor memory usage and look for opportunities to reduce memory consumption:

- Use data structures that require less memory.
- Avoid keeping large objects in memory if they can be processed and discarded.

Improve I/O Performance

For I/O-bound operations, such as network requests or database queries:

- Use asynchronous libraries (like httpx for HTTP requests) to prevent blocking.
- Batch requests to reduce the number of round trips to external services.

Implement Caching

Caching can significantly improve response times. Consider:

- In-memory caching for frequently accessed data.
- HTTP caching headers to instruct clients and proxies on how to cache responses.

Load Balancing

For high-traffic applications, consider using load balancers to distribute requests across multiple instances of your application. This ensures that no single instance becomes a bottleneck.

Profiling and measuring performance are essential steps in optimizing asynchronous applications. By using the right tools and techniques, you can identify bottlenecks, understand application behavior under load, and implement effective optimizations.

Optimizing Network I/O Operations

Optimizing network I/O operations is crucial for improving the performance and responsiveness of asynchronous applications, particularly when dealing with APIs or external services. Slow network responses can significantly impact the overall user experience, leading to increased latency and reduced throughput. In this section, we will explore strategies for optimizing network I/O operations in asynchronous applications, focusing on techniques such as using efficient libraries, managing connections, minimizing latency, and leveraging caching.

1. Understanding Network I/O in Asynchronous Applications

Network I/O operations involve sending and receiving data over a network, which can be a bottleneck for application performance. Asynchronous programming allows applications to handle network I/O without blocking the main execution thread, enabling other tasks to run concurrently while waiting for responses.

Common Challenges in Network I/O

- **Latency**: The time taken for a request to travel from the client to the server and back can introduce delays in response times.
- **Connection Overhead**: Establishing new connections for each request can add significant latency, especially in high-frequency use cases.
- **Network Reliability**: Network interruptions or slow connections can lead to failed requests or timeouts.

2. Using Efficient Libraries for Asynchronous I/O

The choice of library for making asynchronous network requests can have a significant impact on performance. Here are some efficient libraries to consider:

HTTPX

httpx is an asynchronous HTTP client for Python that supports both synchronous and asynchronous requests. It is designed to be fast and flexible, making it suitable for high-performance applications.

Example of Using HTTPX:

```python
import httpx

async def fetch_data(url):
    async with httpx.AsyncClient() as client:
        response = await client.get(url)
        response.raise_for_status()
        return response.json()
```

In this example, httpx.AsyncClient is used to make non-blocking HTTP requests efficiently.

AIOHTTP

aiohttp is another popular library for making asynchronous HTTP requests. It also includes a server component, making it a versatile choice for building APIs.

Example of Using AIOHTTP:

```python
from aiohttp import ClientSession

async def fetch_data(url):
    async with ClientSession() as session:
        async with session.get(url) as response:
            response.raise_for_status()
            return await response.json()
```

Both httpx and aiohttp provide powerful features for managing connections and handling requests asynchronously.

3. Connection Management

Managing connections effectively is essential for optimizing network I/O operations. Here are some techniques to consider:

Connection Pooling

Connection pooling allows you to reuse connections instead of creating new ones for each request, reducing overhead and latency. Libraries like httpx support connection pooling automatically through AsyncClient.

Example of Connection Pooling with HTTPX:

```python
async with httpx.AsyncClient() as client:
    # Multiple requests can reuse the same connection
    response1 = await client.get("https://api.example.com/data1")
    response2 = await client.get("https://api.example.com/data2")
```

In this example, both requests can share the same underlying connection, reducing the time needed to establish new connections.

Keep-Alive Connections

Using HTTP keep-alive allows the client to reuse the same connection for multiple requests, further reducing latency. Most HTTP clients, including httpx and aiohttp, support keep-alive by default.

Example of Keep-Alive with HTTPX:

Keep-alive is handled automatically when using AsyncClient, as it manages persistent connections.

Timeout Management

Setting appropriate timeouts for network requests can help prevent long waits for unresponsive servers. Use connection timeouts and read timeouts to control how long your application will wait for a response.

Example of Setting Timeouts with HTTPX:

```python
async with httpx.AsyncClient(timeout=10.0) as client:  # 10
seconds timeout
    response = await client.get("https://api.example.com/data")
```

This example sets a timeout for the request to ensure that your application does not hang indefinitely.

4. Minimizing Latency

Minimizing latency is crucial for enhancing the user experience in asynchronous applications. Here are some strategies to reduce latency:

Use of CDNs (Content Delivery Networks)

For static assets and certain API responses, consider using a CDN to cache content closer to users, reducing the distance that data must travel.

Optimize Payload Size

Reduce the size of the data sent over the network by:

- Compressing responses (e.g., using Gzip).
- Minimizing the amount of data returned in API responses by filtering unnecessary fields.
- Using efficient data formats like JSON instead of XML.

Batch Requests

If the API allows, batch multiple requests into a single call to reduce the number of round trips. This is particularly useful for APIs that support bulk operations.

Example of Batching Requests:

python

```
async def fetch_multiple_data(ids):
    async with httpx.AsyncClient() as client:
        response = await
        client.post("https://api.example.com/batch", json={"ids":
        ids})
        return response.json()
```

In this example, multiple IDs are sent in a single batch request, reducing the number of individual API calls.

5. Caching Responses

Implementing caching can significantly enhance the performance of your application by reducing the need to make repetitive requests for the same data.

In-Memory Caching

Use in-memory caching for frequently accessed data that does not change often. This can be achieved using libraries such as cachetools.

Example of In-Memory Caching:

python

```
from cachetools import TTLCache, cached

cache = TTLCache(maxsize=100, ttl=300)  # Cache for 300 seconds

@cached(cache)
async def fetch_data(url):
    async with httpx.AsyncClient() as client:
```

```
response = await client.get(url)
response.raise_for_status()
return response.json()
```

This example uses an in-memory cache to store the results of API calls for quick access.

HTTP Caching

Leverage HTTP caching mechanisms by setting appropriate cache control headers in your API responses. This allows clients and intermediaries to cache responses and reduce the number of requests sent to your API.

Example of Setting Cache Control Headers:

```python
python

from fastapi import FastAPI, Response

app = FastAPI()

@app.get("/data")
async def get_data(response: Response):
    response.headers["Cache-Control"] = "public, max-age=3600"  #
    Cache for 1 hour
    return {"message": "This data can be cached."}
```

In this example, the Cache-Control header instructs clients to cache the response for one hour.

6. Monitoring and Logging

Monitoring network I/O operations is essential for identifying issues and optimizing performance. Implement logging and monitoring solutions to track API performance and detect anomalies.

Logging API Requests and Responses

Log key information such as request times, response times, and any errors that occur. This can help you identify performance bottlenecks and areas for improvement.

Example of Logging in FastAPI:

python

```
import logging
from fastapi import FastAPI, Request

logging.basicConfig(level=logging.INFO)

@app.middleware("http")
async def log_requests(request: Request, call_next):
    start_time = time.time()
    response = await call_next(request)
    duration = time.time() - start_time
    logging.info(f"{request.method} {request.url} completed in
    {duration:.2f} seconds")
    return response
```

This middleware logs the time taken for each request, allowing you to monitor the performance of your API.

Optimizing network I/O operations is vital for enhancing the performance and responsiveness of asynchronous applications. By employing efficient libraries, managing connections effectively, minimizing latency, leveraging caching strategies, and implementing monitoring practices, you can significantly improve the user experience.

Managing Resource Limits

In asynchronous applications, especially those exposed as APIs, managing resource limits is critical to ensure that your application remains responsive, efficient, and resilient under varying loads. Resource limits involve managing the consumption of CPU, memory, network bandwidth, and other system resources to prevent resource exhaustion and maintain performance. In this section, we will discuss strategies for managing resource limits effectively, including limiting concurrent tasks, using resource quotas, handling timeouts, and monitoring resource usage.

1. Understanding Resource Limits

Resource limits refer to the constraints imposed on the consumption of various system resources by an application. Properly managing these limits can help prevent performance degradation, application crashes, and service unavailability.

Common Resources to Manage

- **CPU**: Intensive computations can lead to high CPU usage, affecting the performance of the entire application.
- **Memory**: Excessive memory usage can lead to crashes or slowdowns, especially in environments with limited resources.
- **Network Bandwidth**: APIs that generate too much outbound traffic can overwhelm network resources, affecting connectivity and performance.
- **Disk I/O**: Applications that frequently read from or write to disk can encounter latency and bottlenecks.

2. Limiting Concurrent Tasks

In asynchronous applications, it's important to limit the number of concurrent tasks to prevent resource exhaustion. Here are strategies for managing concurrent tasks effectively.

Using Semaphores

Semaphores allow you to control access to a resource by limiting the number of concurrent tasks that can access it. In FastAPI, you can use asyncio.Semaphore to manage concurrency.

Example of Using a Semaphore:

```python
import asyncio
from fastapi import FastAPI
```

```python
app = FastAPI()
semaphore = asyncio.Semaphore(10)  # Limit to 10 concurrent tasks

async def limited_task(task_id):
    async with semaphore:
        # Simulate a long-running task
        await asyncio.sleep(2)
        return f"Task {task_id} completed"

@app.get("/tasks/{task_id}")
async def execute_task(task_id: int):
    result = await limited_task(task_id)
    return {"result": result}
```

In this example:

- We create a semaphore that limits the number of concurrent limited_task executions to 10.
- Each task will wait for its turn to execute, preventing resource exhaustion.

Throttling Requests

Throttling is another technique to manage resource limits. You can implement throttling by delaying requests when certain thresholds are reached.

Example of Throttling Requests:

```python
python

from fastapi import FastAPI, Request
import time

app = FastAPI()
```

```python
@app.middleware("http")
async def throttle_requests(request: Request, call_next):
    time.sleep(0.5)  # Throttle requests to 2 per second
    response = await call_next(request)
    return response
```

In this middleware, we add a sleep delay before processing each request, limiting the rate at which requests are handled.

3. Resource Quotas

Implementing resource quotas helps enforce limits on resource consumption per user or client. This is especially useful in multi-tenant applications where different users might have different resource allowances.

Using Middleware for Quotas

You can create middleware to track resource usage and enforce quotas.

Example of Implementing Resource Quotas:

python

```python
from fastapi import FastAPI, HTTPException
from collections import defaultdict

app = FastAPI()
usage_limits = defaultdict(int)  # Track usage per user
QUOTA_LIMIT = 100  # Set quota limit

@app.middleware("http")
async def enforce_quota(request: Request, call_next):
    user_id = request.headers.get("X-User-ID")  # Assume user ID
    is passed in headers
    if user_id:
        if usage_limits[user_id] >= QUOTA_LIMIT:
            raise HTTPException(status_code=429, detail="Quota
            exceeded")
        else:
            usage_limits[user_id] += 1  # Increment usage
```

```python
response = await call_next(request)
return response
```

In this example:

- We track usage for each user based on a custom header.
- If a user exceeds their quota, we raise a 429 error (Too Many Requests).

4. Handling Timeouts

Timeouts are essential for managing how long your application will wait for external resources, such as APIs or databases, to respond. Proper timeout management helps prevent resource locking and keeps your application responsive.

Setting Timeouts for HTTP Requests

When making HTTP requests with libraries like httpx or aiohttp, always set timeouts to avoid hanging requests.

Example of Setting Timeouts with HTTPX:

```python
async with httpx.AsyncClient(timeout=10.0) as client:  # 10
seconds timeout
    response = await client.get("https://api.example.com/data")
```

This configuration ensures that requests that take longer than 10 seconds will raise an exception, allowing you to handle it appropriately.

Database Connection Timeouts

For database connections, configure timeouts to ensure that your application can recover from unresponsive database servers.

Example with SQLAlchemy:

```python
```

```
from sqlalchemy import create_engine

engine =
create_engine("postgresql://user:password@localhost/dbname",
connect_args={"timeout": 5})
```

In this example, we set a connection timeout of 5 seconds for PostgreSQL.

5. Monitoring Resource Usage

Monitoring resource usage is essential for maintaining application performance and quickly identifying issues. Implement logging and monitoring tools to track resource consumption metrics.

Using Logging

Integrate logging to capture key metrics related to resource usage. For example, log the time taken for requests, memory usage, and any errors encountered.

Example of Logging Resource Usage:

```python
import logging

logging.basicConfig(level=logging.INFO)

@app.middleware("http")
async def log_resource_usage(request: Request, call_next):
    start_time = time.time()
    response = await call_next(request)
    duration = time.time() - start_time
    logging.info(f"Processed {request.method} {request.url} in
    {duration:.2f} seconds")
    return response
```

Using Monitoring Tools

Consider using external monitoring tools to keep track of resource usage and application performance. Tools like Prometheus, Grafana, and New

Relic can provide valuable insights into your application's behavior under load.

Managing resource limits is essential for building robust and efficient asynchronous applications. By implementing strategies such as limiting concurrent tasks, using resource quotas, handling timeouts, and monitoring resource usage, you can ensure that your application remains responsive and performant.

Performance Considerations for Asynchronous Code

Asynchronous programming allows applications to handle I/O-bound tasks efficiently, but it also comes with its own set of performance considerations. Understanding these considerations is essential for building high-performance applications that make effective use of asynchronous patterns. This section will explore various factors that can impact the performance of asynchronous code, including context switching, efficient use of resources, optimizing I/O operations, and best practices for writing efficient asynchronous code.

1. Understanding Asynchronous Performance

Asynchronous programming allows tasks to be executed concurrently, which can lead to significant performance improvements in I/O-bound applications. However, it's important to be aware of certain aspects that can affect the overall performance of your application.

Context Switching Overhead

In asynchronous programming, context switching refers to the process of switching between different tasks or coroutines. While this allows for efficient use of resources, excessive context switching can introduce overhead, particularly in CPU-bound tasks.

- **Minimize Context Switching**: To minimize context switching overhead, keep your coroutines lightweight and avoid blocking operations.

Use asynchronous I/O operations whenever possible.

2. Efficient Use of Resources

To achieve optimal performance in asynchronous applications, it's important to manage resources effectively.

Connection Management

Managing connections (e.g., to databases or external APIs) efficiently is crucial for maintaining performance.

- **Connection Pooling**: Use connection pooling to reuse existing connections rather than creating new ones for each request. This reduces latency and resource consumption.

Example of Connection Pooling in SQLAlchemy:

```python
from sqlalchemy import create_engine

# Create a connection pool with a specified size
engine =
create_engine("postgresql://user:password@localhost/dbname",
pool_size=20, max_overflow=0)
```

- **Use Asynchronous Clients**: For HTTP requests, prefer asynchronous clients like httpx or aiohttp that support connection pooling automatically.

Resource Allocation

Be mindful of how your application allocates resources. Avoid using blocking calls within asynchronous code, as this can lead to performance degradation.

- **Use Async Libraries**: Leverage libraries designed for asynchronous programming. For instance, use asyncio.sleep() instead of time.sleep(), which blocks the event loop.

3. Optimizing I/O Operations

Asynchronous applications are often I/O-bound, meaning their performance is heavily influenced by how efficiently they perform I/O operations.

Minimize Latency

Reducing the latency of I/O operations can greatly improve the performance of your asynchronous application.

- **Batch Requests**: When possible, batch multiple I/O operations into a single request to reduce the number of round trips. For APIs, this can mean sending multiple items in a single API call.

Example of Batching API Requests:

python

```python
async def fetch_multiple_items(item_ids):
    async with httpx.AsyncClient() as client:
        response = await
        client.post("https://api.example.com/items/batch",
        json={"ids": item_ids})
        return response.json()
```

- **Optimize Payload Size**: Ensure that the data being sent over the network is as small as possible. Use compression and efficient serialization formats.

Handle Timeouts Properly

Setting timeouts for I/O operations helps prevent your application from hanging due to unresponsive services. This is especially important in a high-concurrency environment.

Example of Setting Timeouts with HTTPX:

```python
python

async with httpx.AsyncClient(timeout=5.0) as client:  # 5 seconds
timeout
    response = await client.get("https://api.example.com/data")
```

- **Gracefully Handle Timeouts**: Implement logic to retry failed requests when appropriate, but avoid overwhelming the server with retries.

4. Writing Efficient Asynchronous Code

To maximize performance in asynchronous applications, follow these best practices when writing your code:

Keep Coroutines Lightweight

Ensure that your coroutines are lightweight and focused on a single task. This reduces the overhead of context switching and allows for more efficient execution.

Example of a Lightweight Coroutine:

```python
python

async def process_data(data):
    # Process data without blocking
    await asyncio.sleep(0.1)  # Simulate a non-blocking operation
    return f"Processed {data}"
```

Use asyncio.gather Effectively

Use asyncio.gather() to run multiple coroutines concurrently. This is particularly useful when you have independent tasks that can run in parallel.

Example of Using asyncio.gather():

```python
python
```

```python
async def main():
    results = await asyncio.gather(
        fetch_data("https://api.example.com/data1"),
        fetch_data("https://api.example.com/data2"),
    )
    return results
```

This approach allows for efficient parallel execution of the I/O-bound tasks.

Leverage Background Tasks

For long-running operations that do not need to block the main application flow, consider using background tasks.

Example of Using Background Tasks with FastAPI:

```python
python
```

```python
from fastapi import BackgroundTasks

@app.post("/send-email")
async def send_email(email: str, background_tasks:
BackgroundTasks):
    background_tasks.add_task(send_email_task, email)
    return {"message": "Email is being sent in the background."}

async def send_email_task(email: str):
    await asyncio.sleep(5)  # Simulate a long-running email
    sending task
    print(f"Email sent to {email}")
```

In this example, the email-sending task runs in the background, allowing the API to respond immediately.

5. Monitoring Performance

Monitoring the performance of your asynchronous application is crucial for identifying bottlenecks and ensuring optimal resource usage. Utilize logging and monitoring tools to gain insights into your application's behavior.

Using APM Tools

Application Performance Monitoring (APM) tools like New Relic, Datadog, or Prometheus can provide valuable metrics on the performance of your application, including request rates, response times, and error rates.

Custom Logging

Implement custom logging to capture performance-related metrics, such as response times for API endpoints and resource usage.

Example of Custom Logging:

```python
import logging

logging.basicConfig(level=logging.INFO)

@app.middleware("http")
async def log_performance(request: Request, call_next):
    start_time = time.time()
    response = await call_next(request)
    duration = time.time() - start_time
    logging.info(f"Request to {request.url} took {duration:.4f}
    seconds")
    return response
```

This middleware logs the duration of each request, allowing you to identify slow endpoints.

Optimizing network I/O operations and overall performance in asynchronous applications requires a strategic approach that includes efficient resource management, minimizing latency, and employing best practices when writing asynchronous code.

Case Studies: Performance Improvements in Real Projects

In this section, we will explore real-world case studies that highlight the performance improvements achieved through various optimization techniques in asynchronous applications. These examples illustrate how specific strategies can address common performance issues, improve response times, and enhance user experience. Each case study will provide insights into the challenges faced, the solutions implemented, and the measurable results obtained.

Case Study 1: Enhancing an E-Commerce API

Background: An e-commerce platform experienced slow response times during peak traffic periods, especially when fetching product details and user order history. The API was built using FastAPI, but it was not optimized for handling a high number of concurrent requests.

Challenges:

- Increased latency during high traffic, leading to a poor user experience.
- Bottlenecks in database queries when fetching product information and user orders.
- Lack of caching strategies resulted in unnecessary database hits.

Optimizations Implemented:
Database Connection Pooling:

- Implemented connection pooling using SQLAlchemy to manage database connections efficiently.
- Reduced the overhead of establishing new connections for each request.

Caching Responses:

- Introduced an in-memory cache using cachetools to cache frequently accessed product data and user order histories.
- Set appropriate cache expiration times based on how often the data changed.

Asynchronous I/O Operations:

- Switched to asynchronous database calls using asyncpg for PostgreSQL, allowing multiple database queries to run concurrently without blocking.
- Used httpx for asynchronous external API calls to fetch shipping rates.

Load Testing and Rate Limiting:

- Conducted load testing with tools like Locust to identify bottlenecks under high traffic.
- Implemented rate limiting to prevent abuse and manage resources effectively.

Results:

- Reduced average API response time from 500ms to 150ms during peak traffic.
- Increased the number of concurrent users handled by the API from 100 to 500 without significant performance degradation.
- Improved user satisfaction and reduced cart abandonment rates.

Case Study 2: Optimizing a Real-Time Chat Application

Background: A real-time chat application built with FastAPI faced challenges with scalability and responsiveness as the user base grew. Users reported delays in message delivery, particularly during peak hours.

Challenges:

- High latency in message delivery due to blocking operations.
- Inefficient handling of WebSocket connections leading to slow responses.
- Resource exhaustion when handling thousands of simultaneous users.

Optimizations Implemented:
WebSocket Connection Management:

- Implemented a semaphore to limit the number of concurrent connections and prevent resource exhaustion.
- Used connection pooling to manage WebSocket connections efficiently.

Optimized Message Broadcasting:

- Refactored the message broadcasting logic to reduce the overhead of sending messages to all clients.
- Used asynchronous asyncio.gather() to handle multiple message sends concurrently.

Rate Limiting:

- Added rate limiting for message sending to prevent users from overwhelming the server with excessive messages.

Profiling and Monitoring:

- Employed profiling tools to identify slow parts of the code and optimize critical paths in message handling.
- Integrated APM tools to monitor application performance and gather metrics on response times and user interactions.

Results:

- Improved message delivery latency from 300ms to under 50ms, enhancing user experience.
- Increased the number of simultaneous users supported from 1,000 to over 5,000.
- Reduced server resource usage, allowing for more efficient scaling.

Case Study 3: Streamlining an Analytics Dashboard

Background: An analytics dashboard for a SaaS application faced performance issues when generating reports, particularly during peak usage hours. The dashboard fetched data from multiple external APIs, leading to increased latency and slow load times.

Challenges:

- Long wait times for users when generating reports, impacting user satisfaction.
- Increased latency due to sequential API calls to gather data from different sources.
- Lack of caching for frequently accessed reports.

Optimizations Implemented:

Batch API Requests:

- Implemented batch requests to external APIs to minimize the number of round trips.
- Consolidated multiple data fetch operations into single calls wherever possible.

Asynchronous Data Aggregation:

- Used asyncio.gather() to fetch data from multiple APIs concurrently, significantly reducing the total time taken to gather data.
- Asynchronous data processing improved responsiveness and reduced blocking.

Implementing Caching:

- Cached report results for a specified time frame to prevent repetitive data fetching.
- Used Redis for distributed caching, allowing multiple instances of the

application to share cached data.

Database Optimization:

- Optimized database queries for performance by indexing frequently queried fields and minimizing data retrieval.

Results:

- Reduced report generation time from several seconds to under 1 second for cached reports.
- Enhanced user experience, resulting in a 30% increase in user engagement.
- Decreased the load on external APIs and the database, resulting in cost savings.

These case studies illustrate the effectiveness of various optimization strategies in real-world asynchronous applications. By identifying performance bottlenecks and implementing targeted improvements, organizations can enhance user experiences, increase scalability, and reduce operational costs. In summary, key takeaways from these case studies include:

- The importance of profiling and monitoring to identify performance issues.
- The effectiveness of asynchronous I/O operations in reducing latency and improving resource management.
- The value of caching and connection pooling in optimizing network interactions.

As you continue to develop and optimize asynchronous applications, consider these strategies and lessons learned to ensure your applications perform at their best under varying loads. In the next chapter, we will explore best practices for maintaining and deploying your FastAPI applications to ensure ongoing performance and reliability.

Common Pitfalls and Best Practices

U nderstanding **Common Mistakes in Asynchronous Programming**
Asynchronous programming can significantly enhance the performance and scalability of applications, particularly those that are I/O-bound. However, it also introduces complexity and potential pitfalls that developers must navigate. Understanding these common mistakes is crucial for creating efficient and maintainable asynchronous applications. In this chapter, we will explore typical errors encountered in asynchronous programming, their implications, and best practices to avoid them.

1. Blocking the Event Loop

One of the most common pitfalls in asynchronous programming is blocking the event loop with synchronous operations. When an operation blocks the event loop, it prevents other asynchronous tasks from executing, which can lead to performance degradation and unresponsive applications.

Examples of Blocking Operations

- **Synchronous I/O Operations**: Using blocking calls such as time.sleep() instead of await asyncio.sleep().
- **Long-Running CPU-Bound Tasks**: Performing CPU-intensive computations within an asynchronous function without offloading them to a separate thread or process.

Example of Blocking the Event Loop:

```
python
```

```python
async def long_running_task():
    time.sleep(5)  # This blocks the event loop
    return "Task completed"
```

In this example, the use of time.sleep() will block the entire event loop for 5 seconds, preventing any other tasks from running.

Best Practices to Avoid Blocking

- **Use Asynchronous I/O**: Always use asynchronous equivalents for I/O operations, such as await asyncio.sleep(), await httpx.get(), or await aiofiles.open().
- **Offload CPU-Bound Tasks**: For CPU-intensive computations, consider using threading or multiprocessing. The concurrent.futures module can help with this.

Example of Offloading CPU-Bound Tasks:

```
python
```

```python
from concurrent.futures import ThreadPoolExecutor
import asyncio

def cpu_bound_task():
    # Perform CPU-intensive work here
    return "CPU task completed"

async def run_cpu_task():
    loop = asyncio.get_event_loop()
    with ThreadPoolExecutor() as pool:
        result = await loop.run_in_executor(pool, cpu_bound_task)
    return result
```

2. Ignoring Exceptions in Coroutines

Asynchronous programming often leads to unhandled exceptions that can silently fail if not properly managed. Failing to handle exceptions in coroutines can result in unpredictable behavior and application crashes.

Example of Ignoring Exceptions

```python
async def fetch_data():
    response = await httpx.get("https://api.example.com/data")
    data = response.json()  # If the response is not successful,
    this can raise an exception
    return data
```

In this example, if the API call fails (e.g., due to a network issue), the exception might go unhandled, leading to a crash or silent failure.

Best Practices for Exception Handling

- **Use Try-Except Blocks**: Wrap your asynchronous calls in try-except blocks to handle exceptions gracefully.

Example of Handling Exceptions:

```python
async def fetch_data():
    try:
        response = await httpx.get("https://api.example.com/data")
        response.raise_for_status()  # Raise an error for bad
        responses
        return response.json()
    except httpx.HTTPStatusError as e:
        logging.error(f"HTTP error occurred: {e}")  # Handle
        specific HTTP errors
    except Exception as e:
        logging.error(f"An error occurred: {e}")  # Handle all
        other exceptions
```

- **Log Errors**: Always log exceptions to facilitate debugging and monitoring.

3. Misunderstanding Concurrency

Misunderstanding how concurrency works in asynchronous programming can lead to inefficiencies and errors. It's important to recognize that asynchronous programming does not inherently mean parallel execution.

Common Misconceptions

- **Assuming Asynchronous Code Runs in Parallel**: Asynchronous code runs concurrently, but not necessarily in parallel unless specifically designed to do so (e.g., using threading or multiprocessing).
- **Overestimating the Benefits of Asynchronous Programming**: Not all tasks benefit from asynchronous execution. CPU-bound tasks may not see performance improvements and could be better off using synchronous code or threading.

Best Practices for Concurrency

- **Identify I/O-Bound vs. CPU-Bound Tasks**: Use asynchronous programming for I/O-bound tasks (e.g., web requests, file operations) and consider synchronous code or parallel processing for CPU-bound tasks.
- **Use asyncio.gather Wisely**: When using asyncio.gather() to run multiple tasks concurrently, ensure that the tasks are independent and can run simultaneously without dependencies.

Example of Proper Use of asyncio.gather():

```python
async def task1():
    # Simulate an I/O-bound operation
```

```
    await asyncio.sleep(1)
    return "Result from task 1"

async def task2():
    # Simulate another I/O-bound operation
    await asyncio.sleep(1)
    return "Result from task 2"

async def main():
    results = await asyncio.gather(task1(), task2())
    print(results)  # ["Result from task 1", "Result from task 2"]
```

4. Overusing Asynchronous Features

While asynchronous programming provides powerful capabilities, overusing it can lead to code complexity and maintenance challenges. This includes using asynchronous patterns unnecessarily for simple operations.

Common Overuses

- **Making Everything Asynchronous**: Not all operations require asynchronous handling. For small applications or scripts, using synchronous code may lead to simpler and more readable implementations.
- **Overusing Asynchronous Calls**: Introducing asynchronous calls for every single operation, regardless of whether they benefit from it.

Best Practices for Avoiding Overuse

- **Use Asynchronous Patterns Judiciously**: Assess whether an operation genuinely benefits from being asynchronous. If the overhead of context switching outweighs the benefits, consider using synchronous code.
- **Keep It Simple**: Aim for clarity in your code. If using asynchronous patterns adds unnecessary complexity, evaluate whether simpler synchronous code is sufficient.

5. Not Profiling and Monitoring Performance

Failing to profile and monitor the performance of asynchronous applications can lead to undetected issues and suboptimal performance. Without proper visibility, it's challenging to understand how the application behaves under load.

Importance of Monitoring

- **Identifying Bottlenecks**: Monitoring helps you identify slow parts of the code and resource usage patterns.
- **Proactive Issue Resolution**: Early detection of performance issues allows for proactive measures to be taken before they impact users.

Best Practices for Monitoring

- **Use Profiling Tools**: Tools like cProfile, py-spy, and memory profilers can help identify performance bottlenecks and memory usage issues.
- **Integrate Logging**: Implement structured logging to capture key metrics, errors, and performance data. Use logging libraries such as Python's built-in logging module.
- **Leverage APM Solutions**: Application Performance Monitoring (APM) tools like New Relic, Datadog, or Prometheus can provide insights into application performance and resource usage.

Understanding the common pitfalls in asynchronous programming is essential for building efficient, reliable, and maintainable applications. By recognizing and addressing issues such as blocking the event loop, ignoring exceptions, misunderstanding concurrency, overusing asynchronous features, and neglecting performance monitoring, developers can create robust asynchronous applications that provide excellent user experiences.

Writing Maintainable Asynchronous Code

As applications become more complex and rely on asynchronous programming for performance, ensuring that the code remains maintainable is paramount. Maintainable code is easier to understand, test, and modify, which is essential for long-term project success. In this section, we will explore strategies and best practices for writing maintainable asynchronous code, focusing on code structure, clear documentation, testing strategies, and modular design.

1. Code Structure and Organization

A well-organized codebase is fundamental for maintainability. For asynchronous code, this means structuring your application in a way that separates concerns and makes it easy to follow the flow of execution.

Follow a Consistent Project Structure

Adopting a consistent project structure helps developers understand the organization of the codebase quickly. Here's a typical structure for a FastAPI application:

```
graphql

my_async_app/ |  |————————

  app/ |  |————————
     __init__.py |  |————————
     main.py            # Entry point for the
     application |  |————————
     api/               # Directory for API routes |  |  |————————
        __init__.py |  |  |_____
        routes.py     # Define API endpoints |  |————————
     models/            # Data models |  |  |————————
        __init__.py |  |  |_____
        user.py       # User model |  |————————
     services/          # Business logic and service
     layer |  |  |————————
        __init__.py |  |  |_____
```

```
    user_service.py # User-related business logic │ ├──────
  db/                # Database interactions │ │ ├──────
    __init__.py │ │ └──────
    session.py      # Database session management │ └──────
  utils/             # Utility functions │ ├──────
    __init__.py │ └──────
    helpers.py      # Helper functions │ ├──────

 tests/             # Directory for tests │ ├──────
   __init__.py │ └──────
   test_routes.py    # Tests for API routes │ ├──────

 requirements.txt    # Project dependencies └──────
 README.md          # Project documentation
```

This structure clearly separates concerns, making it easier to locate files and understand the relationships between different parts of the application.

Use Clear Naming Conventions

Using descriptive and consistent naming conventions helps improve code readability. Choose meaningful names for functions, variables, and classes that convey their purpose and functionality.

Example:

python

```python
async def fetch_user_data(user_id: int) -> User:
    """Fetches user data from the database."""
    # Implementation
```

In this example, the function name clearly indicates its purpose, making the code easier to understand at a glance.

2. Documentation and Comments

Writing clear documentation and comments is essential for maintaining asynchronous code. This practice helps both current and future developers understand the code's purpose, functionality, and how to use it effectively.

Docstrings for Functions and Classes

Use docstrings to provide a clear explanation of what each function or class does, its parameters, return values, and any exceptions it may raise.

Example of a Well-Documented Function:

```python
async def get_user(user_id: int) -> User:
    """
    Retrieve a user from the database by user ID.

    Args:
        user_id (int): The ID of the user to retrieve.

    Returns:
        User: The user object corresponding to the given ID.

    Raises:
        HTTPException: If the user is not found in the database.
    """
    # Implementation
```

This level of documentation helps developers understand the purpose and behavior of the function without needing to read through the implementation details.

Inline Comments

Use inline comments judiciously to clarify complex sections of code. However, avoid over-commenting, as it can lead to clutter.

Example of Using Inline Comments:

```python
async def process_order(order_id: int):
    order = await get_order(order_id)  # Retrieve the order
```

```
# Process payment asynchronously
await process_payment(order)
```

In this example, the inline comment provides context for the following line of code.

3. Testing Asynchronous Code

Testing is critical for maintaining code quality and ensuring that your application behaves as expected. Writing tests for asynchronous code can be slightly different from synchronous testing, but it's equally important.

Use Asynchronous Testing Frameworks

Utilize testing frameworks that support asynchronous code, such as pytest with pytest-asyncio. This combination allows you to write and run tests for asynchronous functions easily.

Installation:

```bash
pip install pytest pytest-asyncio
```

Example of an Asynchronous Test:

```python
import pytest
from app.models import User
from app.services.user_service import create_user

@pytest.mark.asyncio
async def test_create_user():
    user = await create_user("testuser", "password123")
    assert user.username == "testuser"
    assert isinstance(user, User)
```

In this test, the @pytest.mark.asyncio decorator allows you to run the asynchronous test_create_user function.

Use Mocks and Stubs

When testing asynchronous code that interacts with external services or databases, use mocks or stubs to simulate those interactions. This allows you to test your code in isolation.

Example of Using Mocks:

```python
from unittest.mock import AsyncMock, patch
import pytest

@pytest.mark.asyncio
async def test_fetch_user_data():
    with patch('app.services.user_service.get_user_from_db',
    new_callable=AsyncMock) as mock_get_user:
        mock_get_user.return_value = User(username="testuser")
        user_data = await fetch_user_data(1)
        assert user_data.username == "testuser"
```

In this test, we mock the get_user_from_db function to return a predefined user object, allowing us to test fetch_user_data in isolation.

4. Modular Design

Writing maintainable asynchronous code often involves adhering to modular design principles. This approach encourages code reuse and separation of concerns.

Separate Concerns

Organize your code so that different parts of your application handle distinct responsibilities. This makes it easier to manage and update individual components without affecting others.

Example:

- **API Routes**: Handle incoming requests and define endpoints.
- **Services**: Contain business logic and interact with the database.

- **Models**: Define data structures and schemas.

Use Dependency Injection

FastAPI supports dependency injection, allowing you to define dependencies for your routes. This promotes loose coupling and makes your code easier to test.

Example of Dependency Injection in FastAPI:

```python
from fastapi import Depends, FastAPI

app = FastAPI()

async def get_db_session():
    # Logic to create and return a database session
    pass

@app.get("/items/{item_id}")
async def read_item(item_id: int, db=Depends(get_db_session)):
    # Use the database session in the endpoint
    pass
```

In this example, the get_db_session function is defined as a dependency, making it easy to manage database connections across different endpoints.

Writing maintainable asynchronous code is essential for ensuring the long-term success of your applications. By following best practices such as maintaining a clear code structure, documenting your code effectively, testing thoroughly, and employing modular design principles, you can create asynchronous applications that are not only efficient but also easy to understand, modify, and extend.

Best Practices for Error Handling

Effective error handling is critical in any application, particularly in asynchronous programming where the complexity of managing concurrent tasks can introduce unexpected behavior. Robust error handling not only improves the user experience by providing informative feedback but also enhances the reliability and maintainability of your application. In this section, we will explore best practices for error handling in asynchronous applications, specifically focusing on using FastAPI.

1. Understanding Error Types

In asynchronous applications, you will encounter various types of errors, including:

- **Synchronous Errors**: These occur in synchronous parts of your code and can be handled using traditional error handling techniques (try-except).
- **Asynchronous Errors**: These arise in async functions or coroutines and may need different handling techniques.
- **HTTP Errors**: When building APIs, handling HTTP errors (like 404, 401, etc.) is essential to provide meaningful feedback to clients.
- **Custom Errors**: Creating and managing your own error types for application-specific errors can simplify error handling.

2. Global Exception Handling

FastAPI provides a way to handle exceptions globally through custom exception handlers. This allows you to define how to respond to errors consistently across your application.

Creating Custom Exception Handlers

You can create a custom exception handler to manage specific exceptions and provide a uniform response.

Example of a Custom Exception Handler:

```
python
```

```python
from fastapi import FastAPI, HTTPException
from fastapi.responses import JSONResponse

app = FastAPI()

class CustomError(Exception):
    def __init__(self, message: str):
        self.message = message

@app.exception_handler(CustomError)
async def custom_error_handler(request, exc: CustomError):
    return JSONResponse(
        status_code=400,
        content={"detail": exc.message},
    )

@app.get("/items/{item_id}")
async def read_item(item_id: int):
    if item_id < 0:
        raise CustomError("Item ID must be positive.")
    return {"item_id": item_id}
```

In this example, we define a CustomError exception and a corresponding exception handler. If the error is raised, it will return a JSON response with a 400 status code.

Handling HTTP Exceptions

FastAPI automatically handles HTTPException and provides a way to customize responses based on status codes.

Example of Handling HTTPExceptions:

python

```python
@app.get("/users/{user_id}")
async def read_user(user_id: int):
    if user_id not in users_db:  # Assuming users_db is defined
    elsewhere
        raise HTTPException(status_code=404, detail="User not
```

```
        found")
    return users_db[user_id]
```

In this example, an HTTPException is raised when a user is not found, and
FastAPI automatically formats the response.

3. Use Try-Except Blocks Wisely

When dealing with asynchronous code, use try-except blocks to catch
exceptions that may occur during asynchronous operations. Be mindful of
where you place these blocks to ensure all potential errors are caught.

Example of Using Try-Except with Async Code:

python

```python
async def fetch_data(url):
    try:
        response = await httpx.get(url)
        response.raise_for_status()  # Raise an error for bad
        responses
        return response.json()
    except httpx.RequestError as e:
        # Handle request errors (network issues, invalid URLs,
        etc.)
        logging.error(f"Error while requesting {url}: {str(e)}")
        raise CustomError("Failed to fetch data from the external
        API.")
    except httpx.HTTPStatusError as e:
        # Handle HTTP errors
        logging.error(f"HTTP error occurred:
        {e.response.status_code}")
        raise HTTPException(status_code=e.response.status_code,
        detail="Error fetching data.")
```

This function handles different types of errors, providing meaningful logs
and raising custom exceptions when necessary.

4. Log Errors

Logging errors is crucial for monitoring application behavior and diagnosing issues. Use a structured logging approach to capture relevant information about the error context.

Example of Logging in FastAPI:

```python
import logging

logging.basicConfig(level=logging.INFO)

@app.exception_handler(Exception)
async def generic_exception_handler(request, exc: Exception):
    logging.error(f"An error occurred: {str(exc)}")
    return JSONResponse(status_code=500, content={"detail": "An
    internal server error occurred."})
```

In this example, we set up a global error handler that logs any unhandled exceptions and provides a generic error response to the user.

5. Graceful Degradation

When an error occurs, aim for graceful degradation. This means providing fallback behavior or alternative paths when something goes wrong.

Providing Default Values or Responses

If an external API fails, consider returning cached data or a default response rather than failing completely.

Example of Graceful Degradation:

```python
async def get_user_data(user_id: int):
    try:
        user_data = await
        fetch_data(f"https://api.example.com/users/{user_id}")
        return user_data
```

```
except CustomError:
    return {"username": "default_user", "status": "cached
    data"}  # Return fallback data
```

In this function, if the fetch_data call fails, a default user data response is returned instead.

6. Unit Testing Error Handling

Test your error handling to ensure that your application behaves as expected in the presence of errors. Use unit tests to simulate errors and validate that your application returns the correct responses.

Example of Testing Error Handling:

python

```
from fastapi.testclient import TestClient

client = TestClient(app)

def test_user_not_found():
    response = client.get("/users/9999")  # Assuming 9999 does
    not exist
    assert response.status_code == 404
    assert response.json() == {"detail": "User not found"}

def test_fetch_data_failure(mocker):
    mocker.patch("httpx.get",
    side_effect=httpx.RequestError("Network error"))
    response = client.get("/data")
    assert response.status_code == 400
    assert response.json() == {"detail": "Failed to fetch data
    from the external API."}
```

In these tests, we check that the application correctly handles not found errors and simulates a network error during a fetch operation.

Implementing effective error handling is essential for building robust and maintainable asynchronous applications. By understanding common pitfalls, utilizing custom exception handlers, employing structured logging, and testing your error handling strategies, you can create applications that not only perform well but also provide meaningful feedback to users when things go wrong.

Code Reviews and Refactoring Tips

Code reviews and refactoring are essential practices in software development, especially in asynchronous programming where the complexity of managing concurrency and asynchronous operations can lead to less maintainable code. Regular code reviews help ensure that code adheres to best practices and coding standards, while refactoring allows developers to improve existing code without altering its external behavior. In this section, we will explore effective strategies for conducting code reviews and refactoring asynchronous code in a maintainable way.

1. The Importance of Code Reviews

Code reviews are a collaborative process where team members review each other's code changes to identify potential issues, improve code quality, and share knowledge. The benefits of code reviews include:

- **Improved Code Quality**: Identifying bugs, performance issues, and potential security vulnerabilities before code is merged into the main codebase.
- **Knowledge Sharing**: Facilitating learning and collaboration among team members, leading to a more knowledgeable and skilled development team.
- **Consistent Coding Standards**: Ensuring adherence to coding conventions and best practices, resulting in a more uniform codebase.

Best Practices for Conducting Code Reviews

Establish Clear Guidelines: Define what aspects should be reviewed, such as code style, logic correctness, performance implications, and adherence to design patterns. Provide a checklist to guide reviewers.

Limit Review Scope: Keep code review requests small and focused. Large changes can overwhelm reviewers, leading to less effective feedback.

Encourage Constructive Feedback: Promote a culture of respectful and constructive criticism. Highlight what is done well along with areas for improvement.

Use Tools for Collaboration: Utilize code review tools like GitHub, GitLab, or Bitbucket, which offer built-in features for comments, discussions, and version control. This helps maintain a clear history of changes and feedback.

Review Early and Often: Integrate code reviews into the development workflow. Reviewing code early in the development cycle helps catch issues sooner, reducing the cost and effort of fixing them later.

2. Refactoring Strategies

Refactoring is the process of restructuring existing code to improve its readability, maintainability, and performance without changing its external behavior. It is particularly important in asynchronous programming to keep the codebase manageable as complexity grows.

Reasons for Refactoring

- **Improve Readability**: Asynchronous code can become convoluted; refactoring helps make the code easier to understand.
- **Enhance Performance**: Identifying and optimizing inefficient code paths can lead to performance improvements.
- **Simplify Complexity**: Breaking down large functions into smaller, more manageable pieces makes it easier to follow the logic.

Refactoring Techniques

Extract Functions: Break down large asynchronous functions into smaller, well-defined functions. Each function should handle a single responsibility, improving clarity and reusability.

Example of Extracting Functions:

python

```
async def process_data(data):
    # Original large function
    processed_data = await clean_data(data)
    result = await analyze_data(processed_data)
    return result

async def clean_data(data):
    # Function to clean data
    return cleaned_data

async def analyze_data(data):
    # Function to analyze data
    return analysis_result
```

Reduce Nested Logic: Deeply nested code can become hard to follow. Use early returns and guard clauses to simplify logic.

Example of Reducing Nested Logic:

python

```
async def handle_request(request):
    if not request.is_valid():
        return {"error": "Invalid request"}

    # Process the request here
```

Utilize Async Context Managers: For managing resources (like database connections), use async context managers to ensure proper resource cleanup.

Example of Using Async Context Managers:

```python
async with async_session() as session:
    # Interact with the database
```

Use Type Hints and Annotations: Leverage type hints to improve code clarity and enable static type checking.

Example of Adding Type Hints:

```python
async def fetch_user_data(user_id: int) -> User:
    # Fetch user data and return a User object
```

Remove Redundant Code: Identify and eliminate duplicate code by creating reusable functions or classes.

Example of Removing Redundant Code:

Instead of repeating similar logic in different places, create a single function that handles it.

```python
async def get_user_by_id(user_id: int) -> User:
    # Retrieve user data from the database
```

3. Continuous Refactoring

Refactoring should be an ongoing process rather than a one-time task. Integrating continuous refactoring into your development workflow ensures that code quality improves over time.

Regular Code Reviews

Incorporate refactoring suggestions during code reviews, making it a natural part of the process. Encourage developers to refactor as they add new features or fix bugs.

Technical Debt Management

Maintain a list of technical debt and prioritize refactoring tasks. Schedule time for addressing technical debt in your development cycles to prevent it from accumulating.

Use of Automated Tools

Leverage static analysis tools and linters to identify areas of code that may require refactoring. Tools like flake8, pylint, or black can help enforce coding standards and identify issues.

Writing maintainable asynchronous code is essential for the long-term success of any project. By prioritizing code reviews, implementing effective refactoring strategies, and fostering a culture of continuous improvement, developers can create asynchronous applications that are not only efficient but also easy to understand, test, and modify.

Building a Culture of Asynchronous Programming in Teams

Creating a culture of asynchronous programming within development teams is essential for maximizing the benefits of asynchronous practices and technologies. Asynchronous programming allows teams to build more efficient, scalable, and responsive applications, but to harness its full potential, team members must adopt the right mindset, practices, and collaborative tools. In this section, we will explore strategies for fostering a culture of asynchronous programming, including education, collaboration, communication, and continuous improvement.

1. Educating the Team

Education is the foundation of any cultural shift. Ensuring that team members understand the principles and benefits of asynchronous programming is crucial for successful implementation.

Training and Workshops

- **Organize Workshops**: Conduct workshops and training sessions focused on asynchronous programming concepts, libraries, and best practices. Include hands-on coding exercises to reinforce learning.

- **Provide Resources**: Share articles, books, and online courses related to asynchronous programming. Encourage team members to explore these resources to deepen their understanding.

Example Resources:

- **Books**: "Python Concurrency with asyncio" by Matthew Fowler.
- **Online Courses**: Platforms like Udemy or Coursera often have courses focused on asynchronous programming in Python.

Knowledge Sharing

Encourage knowledge sharing within the team. Use internal wikis or documentation platforms to create a repository of best practices, patterns, and lessons learned related to asynchronous programming.

- **Regular Knowledge Sharing Sessions**: Schedule regular meetings where team members can present their experiences, challenges, and solutions regarding asynchronous programming.

2. Promoting Collaboration

Fostering collaboration among team members is crucial for building a culture of asynchronous programming. Collaboration encourages the exchange of ideas and helps ensure that everyone is aligned on practices and goals.

Pair Programming

Implement pair programming sessions where team members work together to tackle asynchronous programming tasks. This practice can help less experienced developers learn from their peers and improve code quality.

- **Rotate Pairs**: Regularly rotate pair programming partners to encourage knowledge sharing across the team.

Code Reviews as Learning Opportunities

Leverage code reviews not just as a means of catching bugs but as a platform for learning. Encourage team members to ask questions, discuss design decisions, and share insights during code reviews.

- **Focus on Asynchronous Patterns**: During reviews, pay particular attention to how asynchronous patterns are implemented and whether best practices are followed.

3. Effective Communication

Clear communication is vital in any development team, but it becomes even more critical in the context of asynchronous programming, where the flow of control can be less straightforward than in synchronous code.

Use of Documentation

Encourage comprehensive documentation of asynchronous code, including explanations of the logic and flow of execution. Good documentation will help team members understand complex asynchronous interactions.

- **Docstrings and Comments**: Encourage the use of docstrings and comments in code to explain the purpose and behavior of asynchronous functions.

Asynchronous Communication Tools

Utilize asynchronous communication tools (like Slack, Microsoft Teams, or Discord) to facilitate discussions and information sharing without interrupting the flow of work.

- **Dedicated Channels**: Create channels focused on asynchronous programming topics where team members can ask questions, share resources, and discuss best practices.

4. Continuous Improvement

Building a culture of asynchronous programming is not a one-time effort;

it requires continuous improvement and adaptation to new challenges and technologies.

Encourage Experimentation

Create an environment where team members feel comfortable experimenting with new asynchronous techniques and libraries. Encourage innovation and exploration of new ideas.

- **Hackathons or Coding Days**: Organize hackathons or dedicated coding days for team members to explore asynchronous projects or improve existing codebases.

Gather Feedback

Regularly solicit feedback from team members about the asynchronous programming practices being used. Conduct retrospectives to discuss what's working well and what could be improved.

- **Anonymous Surveys**: Use surveys to gather candid feedback about team members' experiences with asynchronous programming and any challenges they face.

5. Celebrating Successes

Recognizing and celebrating the successful implementation of asynchronous programming practices can motivate the team and reinforce the value of these efforts.

5.1 Highlight Achievements

Share success stories within the team, such as improved application performance due to asynchronous refactoring or the successful deployment of an asynchronous feature.

- **Internal Newsletters**: Consider creating internal newsletters or blog posts highlighting achievements and lessons learned in asynchronous programming.

Team Recognition

Celebrate team milestones related to asynchronous programming, such as completing a challenging project or reaching performance targets. Recognizing hard work fosters a positive environment and encourages further adoption of best practices.

Building a culture of asynchronous programming in teams requires a multifaceted approach that includes education, collaboration, effective communication, and continuous improvement. By investing in training and knowledge sharing, promoting collaboration through pair programming and code reviews, and encouraging experimentation and feedback, teams can harness the full potential of asynchronous programming to create efficient and responsive applications.

Hands-On Project: Building a Full-Featured Asynchronous Application

Project Overview and Objectives

In this chapter, we will embark on a hands-on project to build a full-featured asynchronous application using FastAPI. This project will encompass various concepts we've covered throughout the book, including asynchronous programming, effective error handling, performance optimization, and building a robust architecture. The goal is to create an application that showcases the strengths of asynchronous programming while providing a valuable resource that can be expanded and adapted for real-world use cases.

Project Overview

The application we will build is an **Asynchronous Task Management System**, designed to help users manage and track their tasks efficiently. Users will be able to create, read, update, and delete tasks through a RESTful API interface. The system will utilize asynchronous operations to handle I/O-bound tasks, such as interacting with a database and making external API calls, ensuring responsiveness even under high load.

Key Features of the Task Management System:

User Authentication: Secure registration and login functionality for users to create and manage their tasks.

Task Management: Full CRUD (Create, Read, Update, Delete) operations for tasks, allowing users to manage their tasks effectively.

Asynchronous I/O: Use of asynchronous programming techniques to enhance the application's performance, especially when handling multiple concurrent requests.

Error Handling: Robust error handling to provide meaningful feedback to users and ensure the system is resilient to failures.

Data Persistence: Integration with a database (e.g., PostgreSQL) to store user and task data persistently.

Objectives

By the end of this project, you will achieve the following objectives:

Understand the Architecture of an Asynchronous Application: Gain insights into the architectural decisions involved in designing an asynchronous application, including how to structure code for maintainability and scalability.

Implement Asynchronous Endpoints: Learn how to create asynchronous API endpoints using FastAPI, including handling requests and responses efficiently.

Manage User Authentication: Implement secure user authentication using OAuth2 with JWT (JSON Web Tokens), ensuring that users can securely access their tasks.

Perform Asynchronous Database Operations: Utilize an asynchronous database library (e.g., databases with SQLAlchemy) to perform non-blocking database operations, allowing for high concurrency.

Handle Errors Gracefully: Implement effective error handling strategies to manage exceptions and provide meaningful feedback to users.

Apply Best Practices for Testing: Write unit and integration tests to ensure the correctness and reliability of the application.

Deploy the Application: Understand deployment strategies for the application, including the use of Docker for containerization and cloud platforms for hosting.

Project Setup

To get started, we will establish the project structure and set up the initial environment. The following steps outline the necessary preparations:

Create a Virtual Environment: Set up a virtual environment to isolate the project dependencies.

bash

```
mkdir task_management_system
cd task_management_system
python -m venv venv
source venv/bin/activate  # On Windows use venv\Scripts\activate
```

Install Required Packages: Use pip to install the necessary packages for FastAPI, database interactions, and authentication.

bash

```
pip install fastapi[all] httpx sqlalchemy
databases asyncpg python-jose[cryptography]
```

- fastapi[all]: Installs FastAPI along with all recommended dependencies.
- httpx: Asynchronous HTTP client for making requests.
- sqlalchemy: SQL toolkit and Object-Relational Mapping (ORM) system for Python.
- databases: Asynchronous database support for FastAPI.
- asyncpg: An asynchronous PostgreSQL database adapter.
- python-jose: For handling JSON Web Tokens (JWT).

Set Up Database: Prepare a PostgreSQL database to store user and task data. Create a database named task_management (or any name you prefer) and ensure you have the necessary access credentials.

Directory Structure: Establish the directory structure for the project as follows:

bash

```
task_management_system/ ├──────
  app/ │ ├──────
    __init__.py │ ├──────
    main.py                 # Entry point for the
    application │ ├──────
    api/                    # API routes │ │ ├──────
      __init__.py │ │ └──────
      tasks.py              # Task-related endpoints │ ├──────
    models/                 # Data models │ │ ├──────
      __init__.py │ │ └──────
      user.py               # User model │ ├──────
    services/               # Business logic │ │ ├──────
      __init__.py │ │ └──────
      auth.py               # Authentication logic │ ├──────
    db/                     # Database connections │ │ ├──────
      __init__.py │ │ └──────
      session.py            # Database session
      management │ └──────
    utils/                  # Utility functions │ ├──────
      __init__.py │ └──────
      security.py           # Security utilities for JWT ├──────
  tests/                    # Directory for tests │ ├──────
    __init__.py │ └──────
    test_tasks.py           # Tests for task endpoints ├──────
  requirements.txt          # Project dependencies └──────
  README.md                 # Project documentation
```

The Asynchronous Task Management System project provides an excellent opportunity to apply the principles and techniques learned throughout this book. By building a full-featured application, you will gain hands-on experience in asynchronous programming, user authentication, and working with databases while employing best practices for maintainable code.

Setting Up the Project Structure

In this section, we will establish the project structure for our Asynchronous Task Management System. A well-organized structure is essential for maintainability, scalability, and collaboration. By adhering to established best practices for structuring your FastAPI application, you can ensure that your codebase remains clean and easy to navigate.

1. Creating the Project Directory

First, we will create the main directory for the project, followed by the necessary subdirectories and files. This structure will help organize the code into logical components.

```bash
mkdir task_management_system
cd task_management_system
```

2. Setting Up the Virtual Environment

Next, we will set up a Python virtual environment to manage the project dependencies.

```bash
python -m venv venv  # Create a virtual environment named 'venv'
source venv/bin/activate  # Activate
the virtual environment
 (On Windows use 'venv\Scripts\activate')
```

3. Installing Required Packages

Install the necessary packages for our FastAPI application, which will include FastAPI, database libraries, and JWT handling.

```bash
```

```
pip install fastapi[all] httpx
sqlalchemy databases asyncpg python-jose[cryptography]
```

This command installs:

- **FastAPI**: The web framework we will use to build our application.
- **httpx**: An asynchronous HTTP client for making requests.
- **SQLAlchemy**: A toolkit for database interaction.
- **databases**: An asynchronous database library for integration with FastAPI.
- **asyncpg**: A PostgreSQL database adapter for asynchronous communication.
- **python-jose**: A library for working with JSON Web Tokens (JWT) for authentication.

4. Directory Structure Overview

Now, let's create the directories and files as outlined in the previous overview. Here's how to set it up step-by-step:

```bash
# Create the main application directory
mkdir app
cd app

# Create subdirectories for API, models, services, database, and
utils
mkdir api models services db utils tests

# Create __init__.py files to make directories packages
touch __init__.py api/__init__.py models/__init__.py
services/__init__.py db/__init__.py utils/__init__.py
tests/__init__.py

# Create necessary Python files
```

```
touch main.py  # Entry point for the application
touch api/tasks.py  # API routes for tasks
touch models/user.py  # User model
touch services/auth.py  # Authentication logic
touch db/session.py  # Database session management
touch utils/security.py  # Security utilities for JWT
touch tests/test_tasks.py  # Tests for task endpoints
```

At this point, your directory structure should look like this:

```bash
task_management_system/        ├───

  app/        ├───
    __init__.py        ├───
    main.py                    # Entry point for the
    application        ├───
    api/                       # API routes        │   ├───
        __init__.py        │   └───
        tasks.py               # Task-related endpoints        ├───
    models/                    # Data models        │   ├───
        __init__.py        │   └───
        user.py                # User model        ├───
    services/                  # Business logic        │   ├───
        __init__.py        │   └───
        auth.py                # Authentication logic        ├───
    db/                        # Database connections        │   ├───
        __init__.py        │   └───
        session.py             # Database session management        │   └───
    utils/                     # Utility functions        ├───
        __init__.py        └───
        security.py            # Security utilities for JWT        ├───

  requirements.txt             # Project dependencies        └───
  README.md                    # Project documentation
```

5. Initializing the Main Application

In the main.py file, we will set up the basic FastAPI application instance and include a simple health check endpoint to confirm that our application is running correctly.

Code for main.py:

```python
from fastapi import FastAPI

app = FastAPI()

@app.get("/")
async def read_root():
    return {"message": "Welcome to the Asynchronous Task
    Management System!"}
```

This code creates an instance of the FastAPI application and defines a root endpoint that returns a welcome message.

6. Setting Up Database Connection

In the db/session.py file, we will set up the database connection using SQLAlchemy and the databases library for asynchronous operations.

Code for db/session.py:

```python
from databases import Database

DATABASE_URL =
"postgresql+asyncpg://user:password@localhost/task_management"
database = Database(DATABASE_URL)

async def connect_to_db():
    await database.connect()
```

```
async def disconnect_from_db():
    await database.disconnect()
```

In this code:

- We define the database URL for connecting to PostgreSQL. Replace user, password, and localhost with your actual database credentials.
- We create functions to connect and disconnect from the database, which will be used during application startup and shutdown.

7. Implementing User Model

Next, we will define the user model in models/user.py. This will represent the user entity in our application.

Code for models/user.py:

```python
from sqlalchemy import Column, Integer, String
from sqlalchemy.ext.declarative import declarative_base

Base = declarative_base()

class User(Base):
    __tablename__ = "users"

    id = Column(Integer, primary_key=True, index=True)
    username = Column(String, unique=True, index=True)
    password_hash = Column(String)

    def __repr__(self):
        return f"<User(id={self.id}, username='{self.username}')>"
```

In this code, we define a User class that maps to the users table in the database. The username field is unique, ensuring that no two users can have the same username.

Setting up a well-structured project for the Asynchronous Task Management System is crucial for ensuring maintainability and scalability. In this section, we created a project directory, set up a virtual environment, installed the necessary packages, and defined the initial code structure.

Implementing Core Features Asynchronously

In this section, we will implement the core features of our Asynchronous Task Management System, focusing on user authentication and task management functionalities. We will leverage asynchronous programming techniques throughout the implementation to ensure that our application remains responsive and efficient.

1. User Authentication

User authentication is essential for any application that manages user data. In our Task Management System, we will implement registration and login functionalities using OAuth2 with JSON Web Tokens (JWT) for secure authentication.

Setting Up User Registration

First, we will create an endpoint for user registration. This will allow users to sign up by providing a username and password, which we will securely hash before storing them in the database.

Code for User Registration in api/auth.py:

```python
from fastapi import APIRouter, HTTPException, Depends
from sqlalchemy.orm import Session
from passlib.context import CryptContext
from app.db.session import database
from app.models.user import User
from sqlalchemy import select

router = APIRouter()
```

```
pwd_context = CryptContext(schemes=
["bcrypt"], deprecated="auto")

@router.post("/register")
async def register(username: str, password: str):
    # Check if the username already exists
    query = select(User).where(User.username == username)
    existing_user = await database.fetch_one(query)
    if existing_user:
        raise HTTPException(status_code=400,
detail="Username already registered.")

    # Hash the password
    hashed_password = pwd_context.hash(password)
    new_user = User(username=username,
 password_hash=hashed_password)

    # Insert the new user into the database
    await database.execute(User.__table__.insert(),
    new_user.__dict__)
    return {"message": "User registered successfully."}
```

In this code:

- We define a register endpoint that accepts a username and password.
- We check if the username already exists in the database. If it does, we raise an HTTPException.
- We hash the password using passlib and create a new User instance before inserting it into the database.

Implementing User Login

Next, we will create an endpoint for user login, which will verify the user's credentials and return a JWT upon successful authentication.

Code for User Login in api/auth.py:

```python

from fastapi import Depends
from app.utils.security import create_access_token

@router.post("/login")
async def login(username: str, password: str):
    # Retrieve user from the database
    query = select(User).where(User.username == username)
    user = await database.fetch_one(query)

    if user is None or not pwd_context.verify(password,
    user.password_hash):
        raise HTTPException(status_code=401,
detail="Invalid username or password.")

    # Create and return a JWT
    access_token = create_access_
token(data={"sub": username})
    return {"access_token": access_token,
 "token_type": "bearer"}
```

In this code:

- We retrieve the user by their username and verify the password using passlib.
- If the credentials are valid, we generate a JWT using a utility function, create_access_token, which we will define next.

Creating the JWT Utility Function

To generate JWTs, we will implement a utility function in utils/security.py. This function will use the python-jose library to create tokens.

Code for JWT Utility Function in utils/security.py:

```python

```

```
from datetime import datetime, timedelta
from jose import JWTError, jwt
from fastapi import Depends, Security

SECRET_KEY = "your_secret_key"  # Change
this to a secure secret key
ALGORITHM = "HS256"
ACCESS_TOKEN_EXPIRE_MINUTES = 30

def create_access_token(data: dict,
expires_delta: timedelta = None):
    to_encode = data.copy()
    if expires_delta:
        expire = datetime.utcnow() + expires_delta
    else:
        expire = datetime.utcnow() +
        timedelta(minutes=ACCESS_TOKEN_EXPIRE_MINUTES)
    to_encode.update({"exp": expire})
    encoded_jwt = jwt.encode(to_encode, SECRET_KEY,
    algorithm=ALGORITHM)
    return encoded_jwt
```

In this utility function:

- We define constants for the secret key, algorithm, and token expiration time.
- The create_access_token function takes user data and generates a JWT with an expiration time.

2. Task Management Functionality

With user authentication in place, we will implement the core task management features, allowing users to create, read, update, and delete tasks asynchronously.

Defining the Task Model

First, we need to define the Task model in models/task.py. This model will represent tasks in our application.

252

Code for Task Model in models/task.py:

python

```
from sqlalchemy import Column, Integer, String, ForeignKey
from sqlalchemy.orm import relationship
from app.db.session import Base

class Task(Base):
    __tablename__ = "tasks"

    id = Column(Integer, primary_key=True, index=True)
    title = Column(String, index=True)
    description = Column(String, nullable=True)
    owner_id = Column(Integer, ForeignKey("users.id"))

    owner = relationship("User", back_populates="tasks")

    def __repr__(self):
        return f"<Task(id={self.id},
 title='{self.title}', owner_id={self.owner_id})>"
```

In this code, the Task class represents a task associated with a user through a foreign key relationship.

Setting Up Task CRUD Operations

Next, we will create the endpoints for managing tasks in api/tasks.py. These endpoints will allow users to create, read, update, and delete tasks.

Code for Task CRUD Operations in api/tasks.py:

python

```
from fastapi import APIRouter, HTTPException, Depends
from sqlalchemy import select
from app.models.task import Task
from app.db.session import database
from app.utils.security import get_current_user
```

```python
# This function will ensure the user is authenticated

router = APIRouter()

@router.post("/tasks/")
async def create_task(title: str, description: str = None,
current_user: str = Depends(get_current_user)):
    new_task = Task(title=title, description=description,
    owner_id=current_user.id)
    await database.execute(Task.__table__.insert(),
    new_task.__dict__)
    return {"message": "Task created successfully."}

@router.get("/tasks/")
async def read_tasks(current_user: str =
 Depends(get_current_user)):
    query = select(Task).where
(Task.owner_id == current_user.id)
    tasks = await database.fetch_all(query)
    return tasks

@router.get("/tasks/{task_id}")
async def read_task(task_id: int, current_user: str =
Depends(get_current_user)):
    query = select(Task).where(Task.id ==
 task_id, Task.owner_id == current_user.id)
    task = await database.fetch_one(query)
    if not task:
        raise HTTPException(status
_code=404, detail="Task not found.")
    return task

@router.put("/tasks/{task_id}")
async def update_task(task_id: int,
title: str, description: str =
None, current_user: str = Depends(get_current_user)):
    query = select(Task).where(Task.id ==
task_id, Task.owner_id == current_user.id)
    task = await database.fetch_one(query)
    if not task:
```

```
        raise HTTPException(status_code=404,
 detail="Task not found.")


    updated_task = Task(id=task_id, title=title,
    description=description, owner_id=current_user.id)
    await database.execute(Task.__
table__.update().where(Task.id == task_id),
updated_task.__dict__)
    return {"message": "Task updated successfully."}


@router.delete("/tasks/{task_id}")
async def delete_task(task_id: int, current_user: str =
Depends(get_current_user)):
    query = select(Task).where(Task.id
== task_id, Task.owner_id == current_user.id)
    task = await database.fetch_one(query)
    if not task:
        raise HTTPException(status_code=404,
 detail="Task not found.")


    await database.execute(Task.__table__.
delete().where(Task.id == task_id))
    return {"message": "Task deleted successfully."}
```

In this code:

- We define endpoints for creating, reading, updating, and deleting tasks.
- The get_current_user dependency checks whether the user is authenticated before allowing access to task management operations.

Implementing User Authentication Dependency

To implement the get_current_user function in utils/security.py, we need to decode the JWT token and retrieve the current user.

Code for Retrieving Current User in utils/security.py:

```python
python

from fastapi import Security, HTTPException, Depends
from jose import JWTError, jwt
from app.models.user import User
from app.db.session import database

async def get_current_user(token: str = Depends(oauth2_scheme)):
    credentials_exception = HTTPException(
        status_code=401,
        detail="Could not validate credentials",
        headers={"WWW-Authenticate": "Bearer"},
    )
    try:
        payload = jwt.decode(token, SECRET_KEY,
        algorithms=[ALGORITHM])
        username: str = payload.get("sub")
        if username is None:
            raise credentials_exception
        query = select(User).where(User.username == username)
        user = await database.fetch_one(query)
        if user is None:
            raise credentials_exception
    except JWTError:
        raise credentials_exception
    return user
```

In this function:

- We decode the JWT token to extract the username and retrieve the corresponding user from the database.
- If the token is invalid or the user does not exist, we raise an HTTPException.

In this section, we implemented the core features of our Asynchronous Task Management System, focusing on user authentication and task management functionalities. We created endpoints for user registration and login, allowing users to securely authenticate and manage their tasks. Additionally, we set up task CRUD operations, ensuring users can create, read, update, and delete their tasks asynchronously.

Testing and Debugging the Application

Testing and debugging are crucial stages in the development lifecycle of any application, including our Asynchronous Task Management System. Effective testing ensures that the application behaves as expected, while debugging helps identify and resolve issues that arise during development or after deployment. In this section, we will cover strategies for testing our FastAPI application, including unit tests, integration tests, and debugging techniques.

1. Setting Up Testing Environment

Before diving into testing, we need to ensure that our testing environment is set up correctly. We will use pytest as our testing framework, along with httpx for making requests to our FastAPI application during tests.

Installing Testing Dependencies

Ensure you have pytest and httpx installed in your virtual environment. You can install them using pip:

```bash
pip install pytest pytest-asyncio httpx
```

Creating a Testing Directory

Create a directory named tests in your project structure if you haven't already done so. This will contain all our test cases.

```bash
mkdir tests
```

2. Writing Unit Tests

Unit tests focus on testing individual components or functions in isolation. In our application, we can start by testing utility functions, such as those in the security.py file.

Testing JWT Creation and Verification

Create a test file named test_security.py in the tests directory to test the JWT utility functions.

Code for tests/test_security.py:

```python
import pytest
from app.utils.security import create_access_token, SECRET_KEY,
ALGORITHM
from jose import jwt

def test_create_access_token():
    data = {"sub": "testuser"}
    token = create_access_token(data=data)
    payload = jwt.decode(token, SECRET_KEY,
    algorithms=[ALGORITHM])
    assert payload["sub"] == "testuser"
```

In this test:

- We create an access token for a test user and decode it to verify the payload contains the expected user data.

3. Integration Testing with FastAPI

Integration tests ensure that various components of the application work together as expected. In our case, we will test the FastAPI endpoints.

Writing Integration Tests

Create a new test file named test_routes.py in the tests directory to test our API routes, including user registration and login.

Code for tests/test_routes.py:

python

```python
import pytest
from fastapi import FastAPI
from fastapi.testclient import TestClient
from app.main import app
from app.db.session import database

client = TestClient(app)

@pytest.fixture(scope="module", autouse=True)
async def setup_database():
    # Connect to the database and create tables
    await database.connect()
    yield
    await database.disconnect()

def test_register_user():
    response = client.post("/register",
 json={"username": "testuser", "password": "password123"})
    assert response.status_code == 200
    assert response.json() == {"message": "User registered
    successfully."}

def test_login_user():
    response = client.post("/login",
 json={"username": "testuser", "password": "password123"})
    assert response.status_code == 200
    assert "access_token" in response.json()

def test_login_invalid_user():
    response = client.post("/login",
 json={"username": "invaliduser", "password": "wrongpassword"})
    assert response.status_code == 401
    assert response.json() == {"detail": "Invalid username or
```

```
password."}
```

In these tests:

- We test user registration and ensure a successful response.
- We validate the login functionality, both for a valid user and an invalid user attempt.

4. Testing Task Management Endpoints

We also need to test the task management functionalities, including creating, reading, updating, and deleting tasks.

Code for Testing Task Endpoints in tests/test_tasks.py:

```python
from fastapi.testclient import TestClient
from app.main import app
from app.db.session import database

client = TestClient(app)

@pytest.fixture(scope="module", autouse=True)
async def setup_database():
    await database.connect()
    yield
    await database.disconnect()

# First, register and log in to obtain the access token
def login():
    response = client.post("/login",
  json={"username": "testuser", "password": "password123"})
    return response.json()["access_token"]

def test_create_task():
    token = login()
    response = client.post(
        "/tasks/",
```

```python
        json={"title": "Test Task", "description": "This is a
        test task."},
        headers={"Authorization": f"Bearer {token}"}
    )
    assert response.status_code == 200
    assert response.json() == {"message": "Task created
    successfully."}

def test_read_tasks():
    token = login()
    response = client.get("/tasks/", headers={"Authorization":
    f"Bearer {token}"})
    assert response.status_code == 200
    assert isinstance(response.json(), list)
 # Expecting a list of tasks

def test_update_task():
    token = login()
    # Assume task ID 1 exists; replace
 with actual task ID for your test
    response = client.put(
        "/tasks/1",
        json={"title": "Updated Task", "description":
"This task has been updated."},
        headers={"Authorization": f"Bearer {token}"}
    )
    assert response.status_code == 200
    assert response.json() == {"message": "Task updated
    successfully."}

def test_delete_task():
    token = login()
    # Assume task ID 1 exists; replace with actual task ID for
    your test
    response = client.delete("/tasks/1",
    headers={"Authorization": f"Bearer {token}"})
    assert response.status_code == 200
    assert response.json() == {"message": "Task deleted
    successfully."}
```

In these tests:

- We test the full cycle of task management, ensuring that tasks can be created, read, updated, and deleted as expected.
- The tests utilize a login function to authenticate users and obtain the necessary JWT for accessing protected endpoints.

5. Debugging Techniques

Even with thorough testing, you may encounter issues during development or after deployment. Here are some debugging techniques to help you identify and resolve problems in your asynchronous application:

Logging

Implementing structured logging can significantly aid in debugging. Use the Python logging module to log messages at various levels (DEBUG, INFO, WARNING, ERROR).

Example of Using Logging:

```python
python

import logging

logging.basicConfig(level=logging.INFO)

@app.exception_handler(Exception)
async def generic_exception_handler(request, exc: Exception):
    logging.error(f"An error occurred: {str(exc)}")
    return JSONResponse(status_code=500, content={"detail": "An
    internal server error occurred."})
```

Logging errors and important application events will help you trace issues more effectively.

Using Debugging Tools

Leverage debugging tools like pdb (Python Debugger) to step through your code and examine the state of variables at runtime. You can insert breakpoints in your code to pause execution and inspect the application state.

Example of Using pdb:

```python
python

import pdb

async def example_function():
    pdb.set_trace()  # This will start the debugger
    # Your code here
```

Use FastAPI's Built-in Debug Mode

When developing, run your FastAPI application in debug mode to see detailed error messages and stack traces.

Running FastAPI in Debug Mode:

```bash
bash

uvicorn app.main:app --reload
```

The —reload flag automatically reloads the server on code changes and provides helpful debug information on errors.

Testing and debugging are integral parts of developing a robust asynchronous application. In this section, we explored how to set up a testing environment, write unit and integration tests, and utilize effective debugging techniques.

Deploying the Application to Production

Deploying your Asynchronous Task Management System to a production environment is a critical step that requires careful planning and execution. Proper deployment ensures that your application is reliable, scalable, and secure while providing an optimal user experience. In this section, we will explore best practices for deploying your FastAPI application, including environment setup, containerization with Docker, using a reverse proxy, and considerations for cloud deployment.

1. Preparing for Deployment

Before deploying your application, it's essential to prepare your production environment to ensure smooth operation. This includes:

Environment Configuration

Set up environment variables to store sensitive information such as database credentials and secret keys. Using a .env file along with the python-dotenv package can help manage these variables securely.

Creating a .env File:

```bash
DATABASE_URL=postgresql+
asyncpg://user
:password@localhost/
task_management
SECRET_KEY=your_secret_key
```

Loading Environment Variables in Your Application:

```python
from dotenv import load_dotenv
import os

load_dotenv()  # Load environment variables from .env file

DATABASE_URL = os.getenv("DATABASE_URL")
SECRET_KEY = os.getenv("SECRET_KEY")
```

Configuring Database

Ensure your database is set up and ready to accept connections. This may include:

- Creating necessary tables using migrations.
- Ensuring the database is accessible from your production environment.

2. Containerization with Docker

Using Docker to containerize your application can simplify deployment by ensuring that it runs consistently across different environments. Below are steps to create a Dockerfile for your FastAPI application.

Creating a Dockerfile

Create a Dockerfile in the root directory of your project:

Example of a Dockerfile:

```dockerfile
# Use the official Python image from the Docker Hub
FROM python:3.9-slim

# Set the working directory in the container
WORKDIR /app

# Copy the requirements file and install dependencies
COPY requirements.txt .
RUN pip install --no-cache-dir -r requirements.txt

# Copy the application code into the container
COPY ./app ./app
COPY .env ./.env

# Command to run the application
CMD ["uvicorn", "app.main:app", "--host", "0.0.0.0", "--port", "8000"]
```

In this Dockerfile:

- We use a slim Python image for efficiency.
- Set the working directory and copy the necessary files.

- Install dependencies from requirements.txt.
- Define the command to run the FastAPI application using Uvicorn.

Building the Docker Image

To build the Docker image, run the following command in the root directory of your project:

```bash
docker build -t task_management_system .
```

Running the Docker Container

Run the Docker container using the following command:

```bash
docker run -d -p 8000:8000 --env-file .env task_management_system
```

This command:

- Runs the container in detached mode (-d).
- Maps port 8000 on your local machine to port 8000 in the container.
- Uses the .env file to load environment variables.

3. Setting Up a Reverse Proxy

To improve performance, security, and manageability, it is recommended to set up a reverse proxy server, such as Nginx, in front of your FastAPI application.

Installing Nginx

Install Nginx on your server. On Ubuntu, you can use:

```bash
bash

sudo apt update
sudo apt install nginx
```

Configuring Nginx

Create an Nginx configuration file for your FastAPI application:

Example Nginx Configuration (/etc/nginx/sites-available/fastapi.conf):

```nginx
nginx

server {
    listen 80;
    server_name your_domain_or_IP;

    location / {
        proxy_pass http://localhost:8000;  # Forward requests to
        FastAPI application
        proxy_set_header Host $host;
        proxy_set_header X-Real-IP $remote_addr;
        proxy_set_header X-Forwarded-For
        $proxy_add_x_forwarded_for;
        proxy_set_header X-Forwarded-Proto $scheme;
    }
}
```

Enable the configuration by creating a symbolic link to the sites-enabled directory:

```bash
bash

sudo ln -s /etc/nginx/sites-available/
fastapi.conf
/etc/nginx/sites-enabled/
```

Test the Nginx configuration:

```
bash
```

```
sudo nginx -t
```

If the test is successful, restart Nginx:

```
bash
```

```
sudo systemctl restart nginx
```

4. Deploying to Cloud Platforms

While Docker and Nginx can be run on any server, deploying your application to cloud platforms can offer scalability and ease of management. Below are popular cloud platforms and their deployment methods.

Deploying to Heroku

Install the Heroku CLI and log in.

Create a Procfile in the root directory of your project:

```
bash
```

```
web: gunicorn app.main:app -w 4 -k
 uvicorn.workers.UvicornWorker
--bind 0.0.0.0:${PORT}
```

Deploy your application to Heroku:

```
bash
```

```
heroku create your-app-name
git add .
git commit -m "Deploying FastAPI application"
git push heroku master
```

Deploying to AWS Elastic Beanstalk

Install the AWS CLI and configure your credentials.
Initialize your Elastic Beanstalk application:

```bash
eb init -p python-3.9 your-app-name
```

Create an environment and deploy:

```bash
eb create your-environment-name
eb deploy
```

Deploying to Google Cloud Run
Install the Google Cloud SDK.
Build and push your Docker image to Google Container Registry:

```bash
gcloud builds submit --tag
gcr.io/your-project-id/task_management_system
```

Deploy to Cloud Run:

```bash
gcloud run deploy --image
gcr.io/your-project-id/task_management_system --platform managed
```

5. Monitoring and Maintaining the Application
Once deployed, it's important to monitor the application's performance and maintain its reliability.

Setting Up Monitoring Tools
Utilize tools like Prometheus, Grafana, or New Relic to monitor application performance and resource usage. Ensure you log errors and critical

events to facilitate troubleshooting.

Regular Updates

Keep your dependencies updated to mitigate security vulnerabilities and performance issues. Regularly review your application for performance bottlenecks and areas for improvement.

In this section, we covered the essential steps for deploying the Asynchronous Task Management System to a production environment. By preparing the environment, containerizing the application with Docker, setting up a reverse proxy with Nginx, and considering cloud deployment options, you can ensure that your application is robust, secure, and scalable.

Deployment is a critical phase in the software development lifecycle, and following best practices will help you deliver high-quality applications that perform well under real-world conditions. In the next chapter, we will explore advanced topics such as scaling the application, optimizing performance further, and leveraging additional features of FastAPI to enhance the user experience. This knowledge will empower you to effectively manage and scale your asynchronous applications in a production environment.

Supplementary Resources

Recommended Libraries and Tools
In the rapidly evolving landscape of software development, particularly in the realm of asynchronous programming with Python, having the right libraries and tools can significantly enhance productivity, improve code quality, and streamline the development process. This chapter will provide a comprehensive overview of recommended libraries and tools that are particularly useful when building asynchronous applications with FastAPI and related technologies. We will categorize these resources based on their functionalities, including web frameworks, database management, authentication, testing, debugging, monitoring, and deployment.

1. Web Frameworks
While FastAPI is our primary focus, there are other web frameworks and libraries that can complement or serve as alternatives based on specific project needs.

- **Starlette**: FastAPI is built on top of Starlette, a lightweight ASGI framework that provides essential functionalities for building asynchronous web applications. If you need finer control over routing and middleware, Starlette can be a great choice.
- **Sanic**: Sanic is an asynchronous web framework that allows for fast HTTP responses and can handle large amounts of concurrent requests. It is similar to Flask but optimized for async features.

- **Tornado**: An older framework that supports long polling and WebSockets, Tornado is useful for building applications that require long-lived network connections.

2. Database Management Libraries

Asynchronous applications often require efficient database interactions. The following libraries provide excellent support for asynchronous database operations:

- **SQLAlchemy**: While SQLAlchemy is a synchronous ORM, its asynchronous counterpart, SQLAlchemy 1.4 and newer, supports async functionality through its core and ORM layers. It allows for complex queries and relationships.
- **Databases**: An asynchronous database framework for Python that works well with SQLAlchemy. It supports various databases, including PostgreSQL, MySQL, and SQLite, providing a simple interface for asynchronous database interactions.
- **Tortoise-ORM**: An easy-to-use asyncio ORM inspired by Django. It provides support for simple and complex queries while maintaining the async paradigm, making it suitable for projects where ease of use is critical.
- **Gino**: A modern async ORM built on top of SQLAlchemy core. Gino provides an elegant and simple way to interact with databases while being fully async-compatible.

3. Authentication and Authorization Libraries

Securing your asynchronous applications is vital. These libraries can help you manage user authentication and authorization:

- **OAuth2 with FastAPI**: FastAPI has built-in support for OAuth2 authentication, making it easy to implement secure authentication flows. The framework handles JWT creation and validation out of the box.
- **Authlib**: A comprehensive library for implementing OAuth1, OAuth2,

and OpenID Connect. It can be used in conjunction with FastAPI to provide advanced authentication capabilities.

- **Python-Jose**: A library for working with JSON Web Tokens (JWT). It simplifies the process of encoding and decoding JWTs, making it a valuable tool for implementing token-based authentication.

4. Testing Libraries

Testing is crucial in maintaining the quality of asynchronous applications. The following libraries facilitate efficient testing of your FastAPI application:

- **pytest**: A powerful testing framework that simplifies the testing process for Python applications. It supports fixtures and provides an easy way to write and run tests.
- **pytest-asyncio**: A plugin for pytest that allows you to test asynchronous code using the async and await syntax seamlessly. It enables the testing of async functions without the need for callbacks.
- **httpx**: An asynchronous HTTP client that can be used in tests to make requests to your FastAPI application. It supports a variety of features, including connection pooling and response streaming.
- **factory_boy**: A flexible library for creating test fixtures. It allows you to define blueprints for your models and easily generate instances of those models for testing purposes.

5. Debugging Tools

Debugging asynchronous applications can be challenging. Here are tools to help identify and resolve issues:

- **pdb**: The built-in Python debugger. You can set breakpoints and step through your code to inspect variables and understand the flow of execution.
- **pdb++**: An enhanced version of the built-in debugger with better features and more user-friendly interfaces. It improves the debugging experience in Python applications.

- **PyCharm Debugger**: If you're using PyCharm as your IDE, it offers a powerful debugger that works well with asynchronous code, allowing you to set breakpoints and evaluate expressions.
- **Visual Studio Code Debugger**: VS Code provides an integrated debugging environment with support for Python, including features for inspecting variables and stepping through code.

6. Monitoring and Logging Tools

Monitoring your application is critical for ensuring performance and identifying issues. These tools can assist in monitoring and logging:

- **Prometheus**: An open-source monitoring system that collects metrics and provides a powerful querying language. It can be used to monitor your FastAPI application's performance and resource usage.
- **Grafana**: A visualization tool that works well with Prometheus, allowing you to create dashboards to visualize application metrics.
- **Sentry**: An error tracking tool that helps monitor and fix crashes in real time. It provides insights into errors occurring in your FastAPI application and the context in which they happened.
- **Loguru**: A user-friendly logging library that simplifies logging in Python applications. It offers a simple API, powerful formatting options, and better performance compared to the built-in logging module.

7. Deployment Tools

Deploying your application correctly is crucial for its success. Here are tools that can streamline the deployment process:

- **Docker**: A containerization platform that allows you to package your application and its dependencies into containers, ensuring consistent environments across development and production.
- **Docker Compose**: A tool for defining and running multi-container Docker applications. It allows you to configure your application's services, networks, and volumes in a single file.

- **Uvicorn**: An ASGI server that serves your FastAPI application. It is lightweight and designed for performance, making it a great choice for production deployment.
- **Gunicorn**: A Python WSGI HTTP server for UNIX that can serve your FastAPI application via Uvicorn workers. It can manage multiple worker processes, improving the handling of concurrent requests.
- **NGINX**: A high-performance web server that can also be used as a reverse proxy to manage incoming traffic to your FastAPI application, providing an additional layer of security and load balancing.
- **Cloud Providers**: Consider using cloud platforms such as AWS, Google Cloud, or Heroku to host your application. These platforms provide scalable infrastructure, managed services, and built-in security features.

In this chapter, we explored a variety of recommended libraries and tools that can enhance your development experience when building asynchronous applications with FastAPI. These resources cover essential areas such as web frameworks, database management, authentication, testing, debugging, monitoring, and deployment.

Online Communities and Forums

Engaging with online communities and forums is an invaluable resource for developers working with asynchronous programming, particularly when using frameworks like FastAPI. These platforms provide opportunities for learning, collaboration, and support, enabling developers to share knowledge, ask questions, and connect with others in the field. In this section, we will explore several prominent online communities and forums where developers can discuss asynchronous programming, FastAPI, and related technologies.

1. FastAPI Community

The official FastAPI community is an excellent starting point for anyone looking to dive deeper into using FastAPI for asynchronous applications. This community provides a platform for asking questions, sharing projects, and discussing best practices.

- **FastAPI GitHub Repository**: The GitHub repository for FastAPI is an active space where you can report issues, suggest features, and contribute to the development of the framework. It's also a great place to see real-world use cases and discussions around the framework.
- **FastAPI Discussion Forum**: FastAPI has a dedicated discussion forum where developers can ask questions, share experiences, and discuss the latest developments. This forum fosters a collaborative environment for users at all skill levels.

2. Stack Overflow

Stack Overflow is one of the largest online communities for programmers. It's an essential resource for finding answers to specific technical questions related to asynchronous programming and FastAPI.

- **Tagging System**: Use relevant tags such as fastapi, python, asyncio, and asynchronous to find questions and answers specific to your interests. You can also ask your questions using these tags to reach knowledgeable community members.
- **Browsing Questions**: Explore existing questions and answers to learn from others' experiences. Often, similar problems have already been addressed, providing you with immediate solutions.

3. Reddit

Reddit has several subreddits dedicated to programming, software development, and specific technologies, making it a vibrant platform for discussions and sharing knowledge.

- **r/Python**: A general subreddit for Python developers, where you can find discussions about Python libraries, frameworks, and best practices, including asynchronous programming.

- **r/FastAPI**: A growing community focused specifically on FastAPI. This subreddit is a great place to ask questions, share projects, and discuss topics related to FastAPI and asynchronous programming.
- **r/learnprogramming**: This subreddit is ideal for beginners who are seeking guidance and resources for learning programming, including asynchronous programming concepts.

4. Discord Communities

Discord has become a popular platform for developers to communicate in real-time through voice and text channels. Many programming communities have set up Discord servers for discussions, support, and collaboration.

- **FastAPI Discord Server**: Join the official FastAPI Discord server to interact with other FastAPI users, ask questions, and share knowledge. This community is welcoming and provides quick responses to inquiries.
- **Python Discord**: A large community for Python enthusiasts that hosts channels focused on various topics, including asynchronous programming. It's a great place to connect with other Python developers and participate in discussions.

5. Slack Communities

Slack is another collaborative platform where developers can join communities related to specific technologies or programming languages.

- **Python Slack Community**: The Python community on Slack is a place where developers can discuss Python programming, including asynchronous programming techniques and FastAPI usage. You can ask questions, share insights, and collaborate with others.
- **FastAPI Slack Group**: Some FastAPI developers create Slack groups for more focused discussions. Search for these groups through FastAPI community links or ask in the main community for invites.

6. Online Learning Platforms and Forums

Many online learning platforms also host forums where you can interact with fellow learners and instructors, discussing asynchronous programming and FastAPI.

- **Udemy**: Courses on platforms like Udemy often have associated forums where you can ask questions about course material. Look for courses specifically focused on FastAPI or asynchronous programming to find discussions relevant to your interests.
- **Coursera and edX**: Similar to Udemy, these platforms offer courses with discussion forums that allow you to interact with peers and instructors regarding asynchronous programming topics.

Engaging with online communities and forums is an essential part of the learning process for developers working with asynchronous programming and FastAPI. These platforms provide opportunities to ask questions, share knowledge, and connect with other professionals in the field. By participating in discussions on GitHub, Stack Overflow, Reddit, Discord, Slack, and various online learning platforms, you can enhance your understanding, discover best practices, and stay updated on the latest developments in asynchronous programming.

Further Reading and Learning Resources

Asynchronous programming is a vast and continually evolving field, and ongoing learning is crucial to stay updated with the latest trends, best practices, and tools. This section will provide a curated list of recommended books, online courses, documentation, and other learning resources that can deepen your understanding of asynchronous programming and FastAPI.

1. Books

- **"Python Concurrency with asyncio" by Matthew Fowler**: This book provides a thorough introduction to asynchronous programming in Python, with practical examples and a focus on the asyncio library. It covers the foundational concepts and best practices for building concurrent applications.
- **"Fluent Python" by Luciano Ramalho**: While not solely focused on asynchronous programming, this book offers an in-depth look at Python features, including generators, coroutines, and the asyncio library. It's an excellent resource for intermediate to advanced Python developers looking to deepen their knowledge.
- **"FastAPI: The Complete Guide" by James Levens**: This book offers a comprehensive overview of FastAPI, covering everything from basic setups to advanced features such as dependency injection, background tasks, and authentication mechanisms.
- **"Designing Data-Intensive Applications" by Martin Kleppmann**: This book provides insights into building robust applications that handle data efficiently. It covers fundamental principles applicable to asynchronous programming, especially in handling I/O-bound operations.

2. Online Courses

- **FastAPI Official Documentation**: The official documentation for FastAPI is an excellent resource that includes tutorials, guides, and comprehensive API references. The documentation is well-structured and provides practical examples to help you get started quickly.
- **Udemy - "FastAPI: The Complete Guide"**: This course covers FastAPI from the ground up, including RESTful API development, database integration, and deploying applications. It offers practical, hands-on exercises to solidify your understanding.
- **Coursera - "Python for Everybody" Specialization**: This course series by the University of Michigan covers Python programming basics and includes an introduction to web development with Flask. While it

may not focus solely on asynchronous programming, it lays a strong foundation for web applications.

- **Pluralsight** - "**Building Web APIs with FastAPI**": This course provides an overview of building web APIs using FastAPI, covering key features, best practices, and real-world applications.
- **YouTube Channels**: Many educators and developers share free content on asynchronous programming and FastAPI on YouTube. Channels like "Tech with Tim" and "Traversy Media" often have tutorials and discussions related to Python web development.

3. Documentation and Official Guides

- **FastAPI Documentation**: The official FastAPI documentation is the best place to start for comprehensive guidance on using the framework. It includes sections on installation, features, tutorials, and deployment.
- **Python Documentation - asyncio**: The official documentation for the asyncio library offers detailed information on its features, including coroutines, tasks, and event loops. It's essential for understanding the foundational concepts of asynchronous programming in Python.
- **SQLAlchemy Documentation**: For those using SQLAlchemy with FastAPI, the official documentation is a valuable resource for understanding how to leverage this powerful ORM effectively.
- **PostgreSQL Documentation**: If you are using PostgreSQL as your database, refer to the official documentation for in-depth guidance on setup, SQL syntax, and advanced features.

4. Blogs and Articles

- **Real Python**: A comprehensive resource for Python tutorials, Real Python features articles and tutorials on asynchronous programming and FastAPI, providing insights from experienced developers.
- **Medium**: There are many authors on Medium who write about asynchronous programming, FastAPI, and related technologies. You

can find practical articles, tutorials, and discussions by searching for relevant tags.

- **Towards Data Science**: This Medium publication often features articles on Python, machine learning, and web development. Search for FastAPI or async-related content for insights and case studies.

5. Community and Forums

- **FastAPI GitHub Discussions**: Engage with the FastAPI community on GitHub Discussions, where you can ask questions, share your experiences, and contribute to the ongoing development of FastAPI.
- **Python Discord**: Join the Python Discord community to connect with other Python developers, ask questions, and participate in discussions about asynchronous programming and FastAPI.
- **Stack Overflow**: Use Stack Overflow to ask specific questions and find answers related to asynchronous programming, FastAPI, and Python development.

6. Contributing to Open Source

- **Contributing to FastAPI**: One of the best ways to deepen your understanding is to contribute to the FastAPI project on GitHub. Explore open issues, submit pull requests, and engage with the community to gain hands-on experience.
- **Explore Other Open Source Projects**: Look for other open-source projects that utilize asynchronous programming patterns. Contributing to these projects can provide practical experience and expose you to various coding styles and methodologies.

The world of asynchronous programming and web development is rich with resources, and leveraging these will enhance your skills and understanding. By exploring recommended books, online courses, documentation, blogs, and community forums, you can continue your learning journey beyond this book.

Code Repository Access and Usage

Having access to the code repository for your Asynchronous Task Management System project is crucial for collaboration, version control, and ongoing development. In this section, we will discuss how to set up, access, and use a code repository effectively, focusing on Git and GitHub as the primary tools for version control and collaboration.

1. Setting Up a Git Repository

Git is a widely-used version control system that allows developers to track changes in code and collaborate with others. Here's how to set up a Git repository for your project:

Initializing the Repository

Navigate to the root directory of your project and initialize a Git repository:

```bash
cd task_management_system
git init
```

This command creates a new Git repository in your project directory.

Adding Files to the Repository

Add your project files to the staging area:

```bash
git add .
```

This command stages all files in your project directory for the next commit.

Committing Changes

Make your first commit with a descriptive message:

```bash
```

```bash
git commit -m "Initial commit of the Asynchronous Task Management
System"
```

This command records the changes in the repository with a message describing what was done.

2. Creating a Remote Repository

To collaborate with others and back up your code, you will need a remote repository. GitHub is a popular platform for hosting Git repositories.

Setting Up a GitHub Account

If you don't already have one, sign up for a free GitHub account at github.com.

Creating a New Repository on GitHub

Log in to your GitHub account.

Click on the "+" icon in the upper right corner and select "New repository."

Enter a name for your repository (e.g., asynchronous-task-management).

Optionally, add a description, choose whether the repository is public or private, and initialize with a README if desired.

Click "Create repository."

Linking the Local Repository to GitHub

Once the remote repository is created, link your local repository to the remote repository:

```bash
```

```bash
git remote add origin
https://github.com/yourusername/asynchronous-task-management.git
```

Replace yourusername with your actual GitHub username.

3. Pushing Changes to GitHub

After linking your local repository to GitHub, you can push your local commits to the remote repository:

```bash

git push -u origin master
```

This command pushes your changes to the master branch of the remote repository and sets the upstream branch, allowing you to use git push and git pull without specifying the remote and branch in future commands.

4. Collaborating with Others

Using GitHub allows for collaboration with other developers, facilitating contributions, code reviews, and issue tracking.

Cloning the Repository

If someone else wants to contribute to your project, they can clone the repository to their local machine using:

```bash

git clone
https://github.com/yourusername/asynchronous-task-management.git
```

This command creates a local copy of the repository.

Creating Branches

Encourage collaborators to create branches for new features or bug fixes. This helps keep the main branch stable while development occurs on separate branches.

Creating a new branch:

```bash

```

```
git checkout -b feature/new-feature
```

Committing and Pushing Changes from a Branch

When working on a branch, changes can be committed and pushed in the same way as on the main branch:

```bash
bash

git add .
git commit -m "Add a new feature"
git push origin feature/new-feature
```

Creating Pull Requests

Once changes are pushed to a branch, collaborators can create a pull request on GitHub to propose merging their changes into the main branch. This allows for code review and discussion before merging.

Go to the GitHub repository.

Click on the "Pull requests" tab.

Click "New pull request."

Select the branch you want to merge into the main branch and create the pull request.

Managing Issues

GitHub provides an issue tracking system that allows developers to report bugs, request features, and track progress.

Creating an Issue

To create an issue:

Navigate to the "Issues" tab of your repository.

Click "New issue."

Provide a title and description of the issue.

Assign labels, milestones, or assignees if needed, then click "Submit new issue."

6. Best Practices for Repository Usage

- **Commit Often**: Make small, incremental commits with descriptive messages. This helps track changes more easily and simplifies debugging.
- **Use Meaningful Branch Names**: Use descriptive names for branches that reflect the work being done (e.g., feature/user-auth, bugfix/fix-login-error).
- **Regularly Pull Changes**: Before starting new work, pull the latest changes from the remote repository to ensure you are working with the most current code.
- **Review Code Before Merging**: Always review code changes through pull requests before merging them into the main branch to maintain code quality.
- **Maintain a Clean History**: Use rebasing and squashing to keep the commit history clean and meaningful, especially before merging feature branches.

Accessing and using a code repository is essential for collaborating on projects and managing code efficiently. By following best practices for version control with Git and leveraging platforms like GitHub, you can enhance your development workflow and foster collaboration within your team.

www.ingramcontent.com/pod-product-compliance
Lightning Source LLC
LaVergne TN
LVHW052127070326
832902LV00039B/4076